Chris Arend

William L. Iġġiaġruk Hensley was a founder of the Northwest Alaska Native Association and spent twenty years working for its successor, the Inuit-owned NANA Regional Corporation. He also helped establish the Alaska Federation of Natives in 1966 and has served as its director, executive director, president, and cochair. He spent ten years in the Alaska state legislature as a representative and senator, and recently retired from the position in Washington, D.C., as manager of federal government relations for Alyeska Pipeline Service Company.

Hensley and his wife, Abigale, live in Anchorage, where he is the chair of the First Alaskans Institute.

Fifty Miles from Tomorrow

Fifty Miles from Tomorrow

A Memoir of Alaska and the Real People

William L. Iġġiaġruk Hensley

Picador

Sarah Crichton Books
Farrar, Straus and Giroux ◆ *New York*

www.picadorusa.com

For information on Picador Reading Group Guides, please
contact Picador.
E-mail: readinggroupguides@picadorusa.com

Designed by Abby Kagan

ISBN 978-0-312-42936-2

First published in the United States by Sarah Crichton Books,
an imprint of Farrar, Straus and Giroux

First Picador Edition: March 2010

10 9 8 7 6 5 4 3 2 1

To Aqpayuk and Naunġaġıaq (John and Priscilla Hensley), who adopted me, loved me, and taught me the ways of our people. It is from them that I learned the elements of Iñupiat Ilitqusiat.

Quiagipsi apai!

Contents

Additional information about Alaskan statehood and Native land claims can be found online at www.fiftymilesfromtomorrow.com.

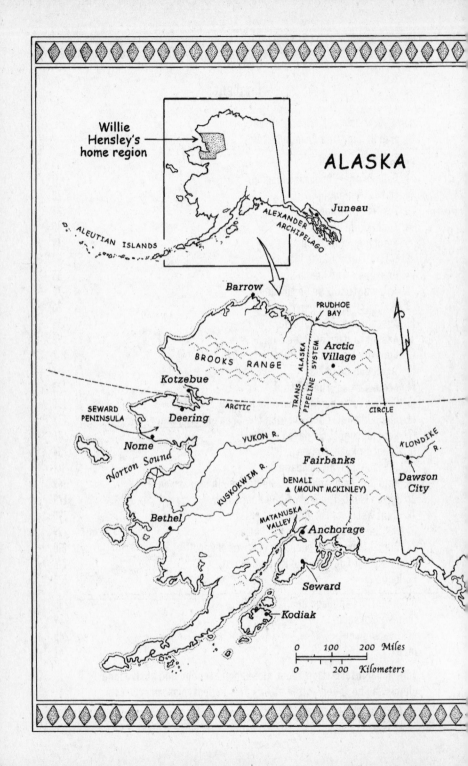

Willie Hensley's home region

ALASKA

ALEUTIAN ISLANDS

ALEXANDER ARCHIPELAGO

Juneau

Barrow

PRUDHOE BAY

Arctic Village

BROOKS RANGE

Kotzebue

TRANS ALASKA PIPELINE SYSTEM

ARCTIC

CIRCLE

SEWARD PENINSULA

Deering

Nome

Norton Sound

YUKON R.

KUSKOKWIM R.

KLONDIKE R.

Fairbanks

Dawson City

DENALI ▲ (MOUNT McKINLEY)

Bethel

MATANUSKA VALLEY

Anchorage

Seward

Kodiak

0   100   200 Miles

0   200   Kilometers

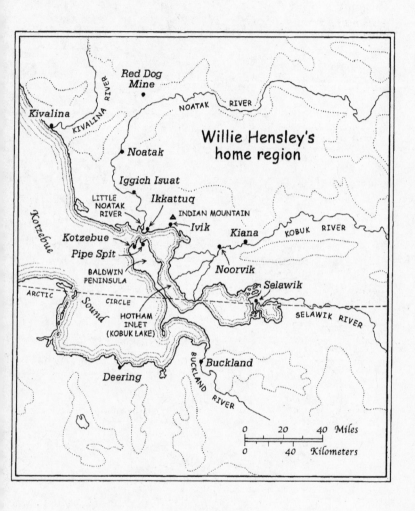

Red Dog
Mine

Kivalina

KIVALINA RIVER

NOATAK RIVER

Noatak

Willie Hensley's
home region

Iggich Isuat

LITTLE
NOATAK
RIVER

Ikkattuq

INDIAN MOUNTAIN

Ivik

Kiana

KOBUK RIVER

Kotzebue

Pipe Spit

BALDWIN
PENINSULA

Noorvik

Kotzebue Sound

ARCTIC

CIRCLE

Selawik

HOTHAM
INLET
(KOBUK LAKE)

SELAWIK RIVER

BUCKLAND RIVER

Buckland

Deering

0   20   40 Miles

0   40   Kilometers

Iñupiaq Writing and Pronunciation
by Lawrence Kaplan

The standard writing system in current use for Alaskan Iñupiaq was designed in 1947 by Roy Ahmaogak, a North Slope
Iñupiaq man, who worked with the linguist Eugene Nida of
the Summer Institute of Linguistics. They adapted the English alphabet to Iñupiaq and added several symbols. With
subsequent revisions, the Iñupiaq alphabet has twenty-four
letters and combinations: a, ch, g, ġ, h, i, k, l, ł, ḷ, ḷ̣, m, n, ñ, ŋ,
p, q, r, s, sr, t, u, v, y. Many of these letters represent the same
sound as their English equivalents.

The vowels are pronounced as in Spanish or Italian, *a* like
the first *a* in English *papa, i* as in *pita,* and *u* as in *lunar.* Double vowels (*aa, ii, uu*) are pronounced long, so they are held
longer than single vowels. Diphthongs are combinations of
two different vowels and are also long. The pronunciations
given here are valid for most Kotzebue Iñupiaq: *ai* and *ia*
both sound like the *ay* in *pay, au* and *ua* both sound like *owe,
ui* sounds like *u* plus *i,* or the vowels in *gooey,* and *iu* sounds

the same as the Iñupiaq *ii* or the vowels in the English *see*. Double consonants are held longer than single ones, so *mm* is a long sound, as in the Italian *mamma*.

Consonant sounds differ from those in English. Here are some Iñupiaq examples:

g   is a soft or fricative *g*, as in *kigun* ("tooth")

ġ   is a back *g*, which sounds like the *r* in French or German, as in *aġnaq* ("woman")

ł   is a voiceless *l*, like the *ll* in the Welsh *Lloyd*, as in *iłiq* ("existence, being")

ḷ   is a palatal *l*, meaning *l* with a *y* sound added, as in *million* or *ila* ("relative")

ḷ   is an *l* that is both palatal and voiceless, as in *sikḷaq* ("pickax")

ñ   is as in the Spanish *señor* and as in *Iñuk* ("person")

ŋ   is a *ng* sound, as in *aŋun* ("man")

q   is like a *k* pronounced farther back in the throat, as in *niqi* ("meat")

sr is like the *shr* in *shrink*, as in *siksrik* ("ground squirrel")

Examples of Iñupiaq words containing sounds found also in English are *Iñuk* ("person"), which sounds like [ín-yuke], *aŋun* ("man"), which sounds like [áng-oon], and *savik* ("knife"), which sounds like [sáh-vik], with an accent mark indicating a stressed or accented syllable. Many sounds have no English equivalent, and so cannot be respelled in this way: *qayaq* ("kayak") sounds just like the English word, but with the *q* or "back *k*" sound. *Niġi* ("to eat") sounds like [nee-ree] but with a French or German "back *r*," symbolized by *ġ*.

Fifty Miles from Tomorrow

Prologue

On Saturday, December 18, 1971, everything changed. It was warmer than usual in Anchorage at that time of year; it was a bit above freezing. But as always during the long winter months in the Far North, the hours of daylight were excruciatingly short. The sun did not rise until just after nine o'clock in the morning, and it set well before three in the afternoon, hours before the start of the big event. As the sky darkened, people began streaming toward the center of Alaska Methodist University, now known as Alaska Pacific University. There were Iñupiat and Yupiat, Aleut and Athapascan, Tlingit and Haida, students and elders, tribal and village leaders, politicians, businessmen, and ordinary citizens. They had come to watch history in the making.

At last the long, tempestuous process of turning Alaska into a real state was about to be completed. The grand poohbahs of Big Oil were poised to start tapping the 10 billion barrels of petroleum discovered three years earlier at Prudhoe

Bay. Big Labor could hardly wait for the construction jobs that would be required to build the $8 billion, 800-mile-long pipeline needed to funnel the black gold to market. And the environmentalists had their sights on the 150 million acres that were promised as protected wilderness areas, parks, and fish and wildlife sanctuaries.

But I think it is fair to say that no group was more anxious that day than Alaska's Native peoples. There were tensions in that room. After all, a centuries-long saga of warfare, treachery, apartheid, betrayal, and hopelessness was coming to an official end. For more than a hundred years, Native Alaskans had waited for clarification of their rights to ancient homelands. And finally, after considerable disagreement, a settlement was about to be announced. The United States Congress had agreed to set aside 44 million acres and earmark nearly $1 billion for Alaska's Natives.

The hundreds assembled stood motionless as the evening's business began. A familiar voice echoed through the room, piped in from Washington, D.C. "I want you to be among the first to know that I have just signed the Alaska Native Claims Settlement Act," said President Richard Milhous Nixon. The new law, he declared, was "a milestone in Alaska's history and in the way our government deals with Native and Indian peoples."

I was there. For five years I had battled to secure our traditional lands. As an unknown graduate student, I had helped to organize Alaska Natives, explaining to all who would listen that we were in urgent danger of losing the lands that had sustained our forefathers for thousands of years. I had run for state office and won, then painstakingly learned the ways of politics. More than a hundred times I had traveled across the continent between my home state and Washington, D.C., where Congress would decide the fate of Native claims. And I had faced the wrath of officials and business interests who wanted to crush those claims.

"Take Our Land, Take Our Life." That was our motto, a phrase I repeated over and over as I made speech after speech on the floor of the state legislature, or lobbied at conventions and church meetings. Our demands were reasonable and just, I argued; people of goodwill must recognize that we deserved a fair settlement.

Alaska has a way of enveloping souls in its vast, icy embrace. For some, the inescapable attraction lies in its pristine rivers, lakes, forests, and glaciers, and in its unbelievable expanses—365 million acres, more than twice the size of Texas. Others are drawn by its enormous resources, the unthinkably rich stores of zinc, gold, timber, wildlife, fish, and oil. For me, Alaska is my identity, my home, and my cause. I was there, after all, before Gore-Tex replaced muskrat and wolf skin in parkas, before moon boots replaced mukluks, before the gas drill replaced the age-old *tuuq* we used to dig through five feet of ice to fish. I was there before the snow machine, back when the huskies howled their eagerness to pull the sled. I was there before the outboard motor showed up, when the *qayaq* and *umiaq* glided silently across the water, and I was there when the candle and the Coleman lamp provided all the light we needed. I was there when two feet of sod and a dirt floor protected us from the winter elements and the thin walls of a tent permitted the lapping waves, loons, and seagulls to lull us to sleep in the summer. There, before the telephone, when we could speak only face-to-face, person-to-person about our lives and dreams; before television intruded upon the telling and retelling of family chronicles and legends.

Still, by the time I was born our culture was already seeing the devastating effects of Alaska's undeniable attractions
for people from what we called "Outside"—anywhere beyond the lands our ancestors had fished and hunted for
ten thousand years. From the first, the Outsiders brought
epidemics of disease that decimated our people. Their massive whale hunts had caused terrible deprivation among
those who depended on whales for survival. In the early
spring of 1899, the business tycoon and railroad executive
Edward Harriman led an expedition along Alaska's coast.
He reported:

> White men, uncontrolled and uncontrollable, already swarm
> over the Alaska coast, and are overwhelming the Eskimo.
> They have taken away their women, and debauched their
> men with liquor; they have brought them strange new dis-
> eases that they never knew before and in a very short time
> they will ruin and disperse the wholesome, hearty, merry
> people we saw. . . . But there is an inevitable conflict between
> civilization and savagery, and wherever the two touch each
> other, the weaker people must be destroyed.*

And as the Outsiders moved in and took control of our
lands and resources, they'd brought another crushing bur-
den: the heavy hand of government over our lives. With Outsider control came Outsider demands. My family and I were
supposed to learn a new language, adopt profoundly different notions of private property; we were supposed to adjust
our communal society to one based on capitalism, self-
interest, and individual choice. Even before statehood, the ef-

*George Bird Grinnell, *Alaska 1899: Essays from the Harriman Expedition*
(Seattle: University of Washington Press, 1995), p. 183.

fort to change Native Alaskans into proper "Americans" was starting up, a joint project of the Christian missionaries and the U.S. government. When I was fifteen, I was cleaned up and sent off to boarding school in Tennessee, where I studied everything but my own people and our history. I swallowed hard, teary-eyed, and left my family for an odyssey that, half a century later, led me to a brick home on Arlington Ridge in Virginia, just a few miles from both the home of George Washington and the White House.

In the intervening years, I learned a great deal about a nation in the midst of a profound transition. I lived in America's South before the explosion of the civil rights movement, and saw firsthand the old, tradition-bound system that was soon to change. I lived through the assassination of President John F. Kennedy. I marched from the U.S. Capitol to the Lincoln Memorial to hear Martin Luther King, Jr.—and later learned of his murder in Tennessee, a state I had come to love. I experienced the Flower Power years and the antiwar movement. I saw Alaska become the forty-ninth state.

I immersed myself in the Alaska Native land claims movement, and helped found the Northwest Alaska Native Association and the Alaska Federation of Natives. I ran for the Alaska legislature and won, and twice became the head of the state's Democratic Party. President Lyndon Johnson appointed me to the National Council on Indian Opportunity, where I served with, among others, George Shultz, Donald Rumsfeld, and Hubert Humphrey. I even became a corporate executive with an Iñuit-owned company in my home area of northwest Alaska, where we worked mightily to uplift our people economically by melding our ancient cultural ways with the modern tools of capitalism.

The world I was born into and the life I lived in my early years will never exist again. Yet, contrary to Edward Harriman's predictions, we're still here. And our spirit lives on. It is our history that is fading, because it's never actually been written down and fully told. I am an avid collector of anything involving the Iñuit or Alaska, and I have scoured countless old book collections. It amazes me: most of the books written about Alaska have been by people aiming to glorify their personal brush with Alaska's magnetism. Most knew almost nothing about Alaska Natives, even after spending a lifetime among us as teachers, missionaries, or bureaucrats. Many saw only the surface of our lives and never understood our inner world. Some focused on the bizarre or contradictory—on our tattoos, our eating habits, our nose-kissing, our smells, our aŋatkut (shamans). In most cases, they did not comprehend our language. The fact that wrenching changes had befallen us and we were working hard to adjust our lifestyles and values to those of the immigrants was lost in the stories they told.

And I began to realize that someday, somewhere, somebody was going to try to tell my story—and through it, our story. So ultimately I decided I might as well try to do it myself.

The Iñupiat sense of propriety includes a strong taboo against blowing your own horn. I didn't want my own people to think that I was trying to elevate myself; we all know that in life, it takes many people to create success. So when I made up my mind to do my best to shine some light on the Arctic and on the story of a people most Americans barely know exist, I didn't hesitate. I immediately called my relatives to let them know what I had in mind so they wouldn't be surprised. They unanimously encouraged me.

The writing itself has been an odyssey. Along the way, I have learned much about myself, my family, and our people. In the midst of the project, I heard that there was to be an auction in Indianapolis, that among the items for sale was a batch of letters "from Eskimos in Kotzebue, Alaska, 1915–1918"—and that six of them had been written by Iġġiaġruk, William Hensley, my grandfather! He had corresponded with Isabel Reed, from Elkhart, Indiana, telling about life at that time. He wrote of the local deaths from influenza, about his six years working with the reindeer herd, about hunting foxes and lynx. He asked her about the world war that was raging. It was as if the spirit of my *ataata*, my grandfather, had suddenly come to life and was speaking to me. I had never known him and knew little about him, and to me, it was like a small miracle.

When I began writing, I knew nothing about the craft, and essentially summoned up the gift all Iñupiat have within them—the art of storytelling. I imagined myself in a small sod *iglu* telling about various episodes in my life as I remembered them.

Honesty is a paramount virtue among our people, and I knew that in telling my story I would have to confront painful issues—something that is not easy for an Iñupiaq man. We are expected to be strong and reserved, and to suffer in silence. Well, I am of mixed blood, and perhaps I can be forgiven for discussing issues that our people usually take with them to their graves.

In the process of writing, I began to see that my story was the story of a hundred thousand Alaska Natives of every tribe, spanning several generations—a story of families and cultures in danger of being obliterated by change, disease, and cultural upheaval. The more I wrote, the more I realized that it was even broader than that. Our story was the story of an entire people across the polar world—and of others as well. I saw the American Indians, who were pushed from shore to shore and yet to this day carry on their identity and culture in parcels scattered across this great land. I saw the generations of immigrants to America who suffered the indignities all minorities face as they tried to fit in. I began to understand how millions of people throughout the world have fought to maintain their identities and unlock the hold of colonial powers on their leaders and resources. We have all tried to find our way amid torrents of change in a world in which others controlled our physical space, as well as our minds, spirits, and identities.

1

Qauġriruŋa: I Become Conscious

I was born a few feet from the shores of Kotzebue Sound, twenty-nine miles north of the Arctic Circle, ninety miles east of Russia, and fifty miles from the International Date Line, at a place shaped by the winds and waves of the Bering Sea. On maps of Alaska, it is called Kotzebue, but the people who have lived there for thousands of years named it Qikiqtaġruk—"small island." It is a beautiful spot, boasting a three-mile beach flanked by willows and grasses and three cottonwood trees. Driftwood floats ashore for firewood, and a wide variety of fish and a salmon run provide ample food. There is ready access to greens, roots, beluga whales, seal, and walrus. And in summer there are berries, many kinds of plants and roots, ptarmigan, rabbits, ducks and geese, and the eggs of seagulls and other birds.

At the time of my birth, in 1941, Qikiqtaġruk was inhabited by about three hundred human beings, primarily Iñupiat, which means "the real people." There were also a few *naluaġmiut.* That's what we called white people—those with a complexion that resembled *naluaq,* sealskin of a lovely ivory color. Most of them were missionaries, teachers, government workers, and traders.

I was born at home, delivered by Blanche, the wife of Abraham Lincoln—Uqailiaq, one of our neighbors. When the missionaries converted Alaska Natives to Christianity, they also gave us English names. Sometimes they simply named converts after themselves. Sometimes they seem to have chosen names haphazardly. And sometimes they named us after famous Americans. I can say truthfully that when I was growing up I knew not only Abraham Lincoln but also George Washington and Robert E. Lee.

It was common for converts to keep their Iñupiaq names as well as the new English versions, and to pass both down through the generations.

Thus, my birth mother—Clara, or Makpiiq—named me Iġġiaġruk after her father, and also gave me his English name, William Hensley. I never knew my own father, a wealthy Russian-born Lithuanian fur trader named Boris Magids. He did not acknowledge me as his son, and he died when I was three years old. To this day, I have no idea who was the father of my sister Saigulik—Frances.

We were *aapaiḷaurat:* without a father. But that was not uncommon among our people, and in the Iñupiaq world of old, birth out of wedlock was not taboo. Since life was so difficult, large families were a source of strength. Blood ties—all blood ties—meant responsibilities and obligations, and a half brother or half sister who lived in another village could prove to be a valuable connection. Such relationships were consciously encouraged, and our culture is replete with stories of young men who grew up as *aapaiḷaurat,* raised by elderly women, and turned out strong and good and prosperous.

By the time I was older, I realized that many of my friends and relatives were in the same boat as Saigulik and me. None of us knew our fathers in our early years, and all of us were nurtured into adulthood by loving extended families. I was a teenager before I discovered I had a second half sister—a fact that no one, apparently, had thought to mention to me. One year, out of the blue, I received a Christmas card signed by "your sister Annie," and was astonished to learn that Annie Iġluġuq Schaeffer, the wife of a man from whom I'd occasionally picked up a salmon as a boy, was actually my real father's daughter, born long before I was conceived.

In my first real moment of consciousness, from when I was only two or three years old, some adult was in the midst of an alcoholic binge and molesting Saigulik, who was four years older than me. We lived in Nome at the time, nearly two hundred miles as the crow flies from the area our ancestors had inhabited for thousands of years. Our mother had moved there, along with her sister Isabel and her stepsister Sarah Adams, to take advantage of the economic boom generated by the Japanese threat to western Alaska during World War II.

My mother Makpiiq had no skills that I am aware of, and I can't imagine what kind of work she found in Nome. Of course, I have no clear memories of those early years. We doubtless lived in one of the cold tarpaper shacks the Iñuit occupied if they were lucky enough to get work in local bars or restaurants or in the nearby gold mines. Without adequate income for fuel, food, and warm clothing, life was fairly brutal. I have only one photograph from this period: a winter picture of Makpiiq, Saigulik, and me in the company of my aunt Isabel and a tall white man whose identity I do not know. I am squinting into the sun, obviously unhappy.

Toward the end of the war, my mother's first cousin Aġnaġaq, whose English name was Fred Hensley, came through Nome. He found my sister and me in terrible shape—abused, malnourished, badly clothed, and living in squalor. When he arrived, Saigulik and I were on the verge of being taken away from my mother by the territorial government that ruled Alaska at the time. Somehow, Aġnaġaq was able to convince the local magistrate that the two of us should be allowed to return to Kotzebue with him.

It was the best thing that had ever happened to me. I do not remember feeling sad about leaving my birth mother, whom I saw only once or twice again all the rest of my life. As young as I was, perhaps I somehow sensed how lucky I was to have been rescued from that squalid life in Nome.

The ride home to Kotzebue on a bush plane is the first event in my life that I recall with clarity. The pilot was a redhead, and his small plane was packed. Among the passengers was a drunk, who stank of alcohol. I was only three years old, and the combination of the stench and the rough air that tossed the little plane all over the sky were too much for me. I threw up.

I distinctly remember landing on the sea ice in front of Kotzebue in the spring sunlight, where we were met by several members of my extended family. One of my new brothers, Auleniq—Isaac Hensley—who was fifteen at the time, swung me up on his back and carried me home. I remember seeing a black cat sunning itself in the window of our small tarpaper house.

That house was one of seventy-five or so on the beach of

Kotzebue Sound. It consisted of one room, about eighteen feet by sixteen feet, plus a small, enclosed entryway, or *qanitchaq*. There were only two beds, really military-style cots, one for my adoptive parents and one for the eldest son living at home. Each night, the rest of us would scramble with blankets or sleeping bags for a space on the floor as far from the door as we could get so as to avoid the frigid wind that blew in whenever someone opened it. There was only one single-pane window, and little insulation.

Kotzebue had no electricity. No lights, no irons, no drills, no refrigeration, no telephone. Our light came from candles, from gasoline or kerosene lamps—or, when there was no money for store-bought fuel, from a saucer and a strip of cloth fired by seal oil. Indoor plumbing was not even a figment of our imagination at the time. Our toilet was a five-gallon "honey bucket" used by every single member of the household, and we had to collect water from the town well up through the willows from the house or from rain that rolled off the roof. It was kept in a galvanized 42-gallon barrel and used for the basics, cooking and cleaning. Rainwater was especially prized for washing hair.

Baths were almost unheard of for some of us children. To Outsiders used to regular bathing, we must have smelled awful—a combination of body and food odors and woodsmoke—but we were unaware of that. In fact, the smells I recall most vividly from my youth are mostly wonderful. There's the scent of the tundra itself, a rich mix of wind and moisture, of grasses, salmonberries and cranberries, and earth. And there's the unmistakable aroma of clothes washed by hand in a tub, scrubbed on a washboard, and hung out to dry in the clean, cold air. In the winter, they would freeze solid: you could actually stand your long johns up and balance them on your outstretched hand.

When Aġnaġaq rescued my sister and me from the abuse and misery of our life in Nome, he was simply doing what a good *iḷa*—relative—would do. I don't think he ever realized how important his compassion was. Aġnaġaq took Saigulik and me from an environment that was unhealthy, unsafe, and overwhelmingly Western to a home in the traditional environment where we learned to contribute our energies to the daily tasks of survival. We learned precious ancient lessons of cooperation, hard work, honesty, sharing, and humor—the very values that enabled me to make the transition from that old way of life to the modern world.

Winters in my homeland are nine months long, and in the dead of the season the "days" are really twenty-four-hour nights; the weak, wintry sun rarely edges above the horizon. On many winter days during my childhood, the wind blew so hard that we could not go outdoors. We would hunker down and wait until the wind died. When it got really cold—down around minus fifty or sixty degrees—we called it *itraliq*, meaning "bitter cold, so cold it hurts." When it got that cold, there was virtually no wind. Under those conditions, the safest thing to do was to stay put until the weather eased. I remember three weeks one year when the temperature never rose above minus forty. Planes stopped flying because the oil would congeal, schoolchildren on team trips got stranded far from home, and elders began to run out of heating oil and wood. At times like that, the people had to pull together and make sure everyone was safe. Any exposed skin rapidly turned white, the sign of frostbite. People lost limbs—and lives. If you worked up a sweat in the frigid cold, you'd begin to freeze the moment your body started to cool. There was very little room for error under those conditions.

I think of those early years of my life as the twilight of the Stone Age. We lived the traditional, seminomadic life our ancestors had lived for thousands of years, always engaged in *iñuuniaq*, the serious business of staying alive. Survival was our primary concern. You could fall through the ice, have an accident along the trail behind the dog team, trip and fatally fire a weapon, cut yourself seriously with an ax while chopping wood or with a knife while skinning an animal. You could get lost in a howling snowstorm or fall from a boat and drown. You could get mauled by a bear or charged by an enraged moose. It was a life of cold and constant effort, but we reaped the bounty nature provided. We culled fish from the sea, game from the hills, birds from the skies, and berries and other plant foods from the tundra, and stored everything carefully so that we had enough when the fearsome winter made fishing and hunting impossible and the plants had disappeared until spring. There was always the possibility that the animal life on which we depended would not be plentiful enough.

It was the primal lesson, drilled into me from my youngest days with my new family: the land and the sea were central to our lives.

2

Iḷatka: My Family

It is difficult to overstate the importance of family in the Iñu-piaq world. In the time before our contact with places and people beyond Alaska, it was said that if you wandered beyond the traditional boundaries of your own group—boundaries forged over centuries of common use and occasional warfare with neighboring groups—your life was in danger. To be banished, the punishment for committing some truly outrageous crime, was hell, the equivalent of being ejected from the human race. Suddenly, like an animal, an exile had to fend for himself, with no one to protect and help him.

By contrast, to belong to the bosom of a family, in spite of all the dangers in our frigid universe, meant protection, aid—and more: a continuity in time and place. There are few people in America who can say that their forebears were here ten thousand years ago. That is a powerful feeling. To know that your ancestors played with the same rocks, looked at the same mountains, paddled the same rivers, smelled the same campfire smoke, chased the same game, and camped at the same fork in the river gives you a sense of belonging that is indelible. Just digging a posthole for your dog might unearth an ivory harpoon head or a flint scraper, and suddenly you hold something that your forebears used millennia ago.

Our extended families, from the most grizzled grandfather to the youngest infant, and those between, were extremely close. After all, we were together day in, day out, year after year. We followed the food wherever it was to be found. We traveled together with the dogs, we fished and hunted together, we picked berries and skinned seals and caribou—always together. In our sod houses and tents, we could see each other's breath, hear the sniffles and farts and heavy breathing. We were acutely aware of the quirks, weaknesses, and strengths of every family member, knowledge that could mean the difference between life and death; for instance, if we knew someone was not particularly trustworthy, we would never depend on his word in a situation where lives or precious resources could be at stake. And we gloried in our shared experiences. We would regale each other with the humorous events of our own time—and also those of our parents' and grandparents' generations.

The head of our family was Aqpayuk, my mother's uncle. He was born in 1893, four years before Quaker missionaries came to Kotzebue from Whittier, California. As part of their mission to "civilize" their charges in the Alaskan Territory, the Quakers gave Aqpayuk an English name—John Hensley—along with a new religion.

Before Aqpayuk and Naungaġiaq (named Priscilla by the missionaries) were married in 1912, he built the small frame house near the shore in Kotzebue and dug a *siġluaq*—ice cellar—for the seals and other wild game he would hunt. It was there that they proceeded to raise their large family.

First came a daughter, Unaliiuqutaq (Jessie), then Aġnaġaq (Fred), Tiliiktaq (William), Umiivik (James), Iġvaluk (Ruby), Saqik (John), Auleniq (Isaac), and Niŋaugaġraq (Aaron), the youngest, who was about ten years older than me. Over the years, Nauŋaġiaq and Aqpayuk took in other members of their extended family, including, of course, my sister and me. By the time Saigulik and I arrived on the scene, Unaliiuqutaq had moved away and Iġvaluk had died. But there were often seven or more of us living in that little house.

By far the single most important person to me in my new family was my new mother, Nauŋaġiaq. Only an inch or two over five feet tall, strong and tough yet gentle and widely beloved, Nauŋaġiaq doted on me when I was little, covering me with warm furs, tucking me carefully into the sled when we traveled, carrying me with her wherever she went. She taught me much of the old language and the ways of our elders. It was from her that I learned much of what I know about our people and their values.

Back in the 1960s, when tape-recording messages became the rage among our people who couldn't write very well, she made a tape that told her story. In the spring of 1895, her parents were traveling north by dog team from Kotzebue to Kivalina or Tikigaq (now called Point Hope), probably for the bowhead whaling season. Nauŋaġiaq was born along the way. But when her mother and father found she was a girl, Nauŋaġiaq recounted, they considered leaving her behind to die. They already had one daughter, then eight years old, and felt that they did not need another. Although hunters needed wives (grown women, as "*iglu*-keepers," were invaluable working companions), little girls simply did not have the physical strength needed to contribute to the family welfare; they were dependent mouths that had to be fed, and thus a drain on scarce resources. What Nauŋaġiaq's parents wanted was a son to help them in their struggle for survival and to assure their security in old age. And so they weighed infanticide.

Fortunately, a childless couple was traveling with them. The wife, Siichiaq, longed for children of her own, and when her husband, Umiivik, was away on a short hunting trip, she took the unwanted baby girl. When her spouse Umiivik returned, he agreed to keep Naunġaġiaq. Had they not adopted her, I don't know what would have become of me.

My new father, Aqpayuk—John Hensley—had beautiful teeth, a tremendous laugh, and a wonderful sense of humor. One of my cousins tells a family story that perfectly describes his style.

Aqpayuk and Naunġaġiaq's eldest daughter, Jessie, had married a white man named Pete Lee. Pete, who had been married three times before, was about fifteen years older than his father-in-law. Those two men were from entirely different worlds. Aqpayuk was very traditional. He almost always wore a hooded calico parka in the summer, knew just a little English, and like most Iñupiat, tended to be very indirect, sometimes almost opaque. Pete, of Italian extraction, ran a pool hall in town, and sold candy, cigarettes, and soda pop. He always wore a Jimmy Carter–style cardigan and a brimmed hat, and being a businessman, he always had money.

Although Aqpayuk didn't like to ask for Pete's help, sometimes he had no choice. One spring Aqpayuk really wanted to go duck hunting. It was the first chance for a change of diet after a winter of rabbits, fish, and ptarmigan. But he did not have a single shell for his shotgun. So Aqpayuk visited his son-in-law at his home in Kotzebue. They had a little tea and chitchatted about nothing in particular. This was a game they had played before.

Finally Aqpayuk said, "Pete, lotsa ducks flyin'."

"Ya," said Pete, and continued to drink his tea.

"Up toward mouth of Noatak," said Aqpayuk.

"Ah-huh," said Pete.

After a long silence, Aqpayuk spoke again: "Got no shells."

Pete dug in his pocket and handed five dollars to Aqpayuk, who wasted no time. He headed to Ferguson's Store for ammunition, jumped in his *qayaq*, and paddled several miles across the channel to the Noatak River area. In no time, he had filled the *qayaq* with ducks and geese—so many that when he returned to town a few days later, the *qayaq* could barely float.

Again, Aqpayuk went to visit Pete. This time, he and his son-in-law sipped coffee. Finally Pete said, "It sure would be nice to have some goose soup."

"Ya," said Aqpayuk, and continued to drink his coffee.

After a pause, Pete spoke again, holding his cup with both bony, nicotine-stained hands: "I hear they're catching geese up toward Noatak."

"Ya," Aqpayuk replied. "That's what they say."

Then he just sat there, silent, sipping his coffee and gazing off into middle space, his face revealing nothing of what he was thinking. Finally Pete couldn't stand it anymore. "John—can I have a goose?" he asked outright. Aqpayuk had been waiting for that question. Without missing a beat, he said, "Two dollars apiece!"

For an instant Pete looked shocked. Then Aqpayuk burst out laughing. Needless to say, he was more than happy to share his generous catch with Pete, Jessie, and their daughter Sophie.

Nauṅġaġiaq and Aqpayuk were very religious. They had been converted to Christianity by the Quakers, although I know they never abandoned the reverence for nature's power and respect for traditional legends that had inspired their ancestors. They particularly loved to sing hymns, which they translated into Iñupiaq, and our Roman Catholic neighbors in Kotzebue still remember the joyful melodies that wafted from our shack as they sang the Lord's praises.

But apart from their conversion to this new religion, my new parents lived a very traditional Iñupiat life. They preferred to spend most of their time out in the country—"at camp," as we called it. Being in town was exciting, but it had its drawbacks. For one thing, living there required cash, which was hard to come by. So for most of the year, my family found it more convenient to live at camp about fifteen miles north of town, at Ikkattuq, a small creek on the delta of the Noatak River. We were often there for months on end, broken only by an occasional trip to Kotzebue for Thanksgiving and Christmas or to buy needed supplies.

When it was time to move to camp, usually in the spring, Aqpayuk and Nauṅġaġiaq spent days preparing. If we were planning to be gone until the ice froze, they had to make sure that we packed everything we would need for five or six months far from any store. Aqpayuk, a hunter first and foremost, made sure the rifles and shotguns were cleaned and oiled and bought as much ammunition as we could afford. Our people had long before traded in their traditional lances and bows and arrows. They'd first gotten guns from Russian traders and had found them an instant boon to the community, allowing individual hunters to be far more productive than in earlier days. Aqpayuk would pack his favorite hunting knife, pocketknife, and telescope and make certain his toolbox was complete. He organized the *qayaq*, sleds, dog harnesses and chains, rope, fishnets, snare wire, axes and ice diggers, or *tuuqs*, plus traps of various sizes and drying frames for muskrat and mink skins.

Naunġaġiaq meanwhile concentrated on clothing, food preparation, and household necessities. She had to pack her assortment of *ulus*—women's knives—for sewing and skinning seals, beluga, muskrats, caribou, and any other game we might encounter. She would bring wooden barrels for berries and seal oil and animal skins and cloth for making mukluks, mittens, parkas, and hats. And she'd pack her favorite *kiiġvik* (cutting board) and the special *ikuun* (skinscraper) that had been carved to fit her hand. She also brought the Bible and hymnal, the pots and pans, the matches and Coleman lamp mantles, the sleeping bags and blankets, the washbasin, and the few plates, bowls, spoons, and ladles we used. Finally, there was the food we would not be able to trap, shoot, or net for ourselves out in camp: salt and pepper, sugar, coffee, tea, oatmeal, rice, beans, macaroni, canned milk, *qaqqulaaq* (pilot bread), onions, potatoes—and, if we could afford it, a slab of bacon.

The rest of us brought our own special items—knives, comic books, games, tobacco. We packed warm winter gear and slickers and boots, if we had them; we were quite poor, so sometimes we didn't have enough for everyone. We also took skates so we could get around after the water froze, and the radio, if it was working.

In the years before we had a boat of our own, Aqpayuk and Naunġaġiaq would arrange a ride to Ikkattuq with the *umialik*—"the man who owned the boat." When I was little, the *umialik* was Qaluraq, and he called his boat *Pauline*. It took an enormous amount of work to build a boat, and Qaluraq's seemed huge to us, nearly thirty feet long. It had lovely curves and a cabin that extended to the gunwales, but there were a few inches on either side of the cabin where you could walk, and a small railing. Qaluraq had a 60-horsepower inboard engine that drove a propeller; the steering was done by hand on a tiller in the stern. It was a great improvement over the old days, when we relied on muscle power to row our boats and pull them upstream to camp.

On the day we left for camp, Aqpayuk and Naunġaġiaq would rise unusually early. I could hear them as they sat up in bed, prayed quietly, then made coffee. They always stepped outside to look at the sky and check the wind to make sure the weather was favorable for the trip. Then it was time to carry our belongings down to the beach, where Aqpayuk and Qaluraq supervised the loading of the boat. By now the dogs would be in a frenzy, eager to be loaded up, and by the time my brothers finished hauling everything on board, from tent poles and stoves to provisions—and dogs— Qaluraq's boat would be sunk pretty deep in the water from the weight. It was quite a sight. As we shoved off, everyone along the beach would be whistling and shouting, wishing us well.

Qaluraq would sit at the tiller, Aqpayuk beside him. In true self-deprecating Iñupiaq fashion, the *umialik* would modestly demean his vessel. It was "too slow," he would say. Aqpayuk would immediately protest. *"Nakuuruq,"* he said. *"Sukattuq."* (It's quite good. It's fast.)

I always avoided the closed-in petroleum smell of the cabin, and instead sat on top to watch the world go by, trying to spot geese, seals, beluga whales, caribou, and swans as we headed up the inlet toward Ikkattuq. After three or four hours, having rounded Lockhart Point, we would turn toward the shore. *Ikkattuq* means "it's shallow," and the place more than lives up to its name. We would anchor the heavily laden vessel offshore and then haul everything in by hand or with the help of the small dory we kept at camp.

After we had pitched the tents and chained the dogs to posts beaten into the ground, Naungagiaq would prepare a meal of tea and crackers, dried fish and meat and seal oil—perhaps some duck soup, too—to celebrate our arrival. Then Qaluraq would climb back onto his boat and head back to Kotzebue, leaving the rest of us to prepare for the months ahead at one of my favorite places on the face of the earth.

3

Ikkattuq: At Camp

Ikkattuq is a beautiful area, rich in fish, game, birds, and the plant life we needed to survive. Along the creek there are stands of alder, and just a few miles upriver are great forests. (In Kotzebue, there were hardly any trees.) Our days, in those short spring and summer months, were spent preparing for the winter. The men hunted and trapped, taking muskrats by the hundreds. The women skinned them, and we eventually ate the meat, roasted or cooked into stews. Meanwhile, the muskrat pelts were stretched on special frames that had been carved during the winter months and allowed to dry—a process that took four or five days, depending on the weather. Once dried, the pelts were tied together in bundles and placed in a small cache high off the ground so weasels and mice could not reach them. There they awaited transport to Kotzebue, where we sold them for cash to buy store-bought goods or to pay down the credit that had piled up during the winter.

The summer run of chum or dog salmon provided an opportunity to catch hundreds, even thousands of fish. We dried some for human and dog food during the winter, and sold the rest to the stores in town for resale. We would pick *quaġaq* (sour dock), a nutritious plant that grew along the banks of lakes and rivers. That fresh *quaġaq* was a wonderful change from the winter diet. A special treat, one of the supreme dishes in the Iñupiaq world, was the liver of trout or whitefish mixed with *quaġaq* and cranberries. We also preserved plenty of *quaġaq* for winter in sealskin pokes. We caught and preserved sheefish and whitefish, and as we roamed about hunting ducks and geese, we reveled in the ripening of the salmonberries, blueberries, blackberries, and cranberries. Berries were vital foodstuff—our winter source of vitamins and sweets. Once the berries were ripe, the whole family would start filling containers. Naunġaġiaq would wait for a nice stiff breeze, then take off her parka and lay it on the ground. She would lift all the berries we had picked high over her head and pour them into the parka, letting the breeze blow away the *sanik*—the leaves and grasses we'd accumulated along with the berries. We carried the berries back to the tent, where they would be stored in wooden barrels for winter use alongside the seal oil and dried meat and fish; as the cold weather settled in, all these supplies froze solid, preserving them for our winter needs.

From the time you could walk, everyone worked. Not always productively, of course. When I was young, I mostly ate all the berries I picked. Still, it was expected that all would join in the simpler tasks necessary for survival. Even a three-year-old could carry wood to the fire. As soon as I had any strength at all, I started chopping wood, hauling drinking water from the well, fetching tools, bailing out the boat, feeding the dogs, helping to check the fishnets and hang the fish for drying, even helping to cook the beluga *maktak* and meat.

Today one of my favorite foods is osso buco, the shank of lamb, pork, or veal. I love the gristle and marrow, and I know that taste comes from those early years in the Arctic. When caribou was caught, nothing went to waste. The *patiq*—the marrow from the leg bones—was a great delicacy. It was slick and rich—nutritious, too—and you might break the bones and enjoy it right away, or you might cook the bones and use a long, thin piece of wood to coax out the juicy treat.

In the Iñupiaq world, of course, animal fat was far more than a tasty indulgence. It was absolutely necessary for energy and survival in that fierce environment. Our primary spring quarry was sea mammals, particularly the bearded seal, or *ugruk*. Their oil—the defining fluid of Iñupiat life—was consumed at almost every meal and also used to preserve blubber, greens, dried fish, cooked seal intestines, and other foods. As soon as the seals began to sun themselves on the spring ice next to open water, we hunted them. We shot them, hauled them to shore, loaded them on sleds, and took them back to camp by dog team.

Then the women would take control, choosing the *ulus* best suited for butchering an animal the size of a seal. In ancient times, those knives were handmade of slate, flint, or jade. When I was growing up, they were usually fashioned from the light steel of a crosscut saw, which holds an excellent edge. The handle might be made of ivory, wood, or bone, and it was often custom-fitted to the hand of the owner.

A woman would slice into the skin and blubber at the seal's anus, and in one smooth motion would draw her *ulu* all the way up to the animal's throat. In a matter of minutes she would have cut clear around the neck, flippers, and tail, separating the skin and three-inch-thick layer of blubber from the muscles underneath. Later, the blubber would be separated from the skin and cut into small pieces to render, at room temperature, into seal oil. Before we had easy access to wooden barrels for storing our meat we used the skin of the seal itself. The women carefully separated the hide from the blubber, making sure to keep it airtight. Then they inverted the hide, dried it, and cleaned it for use as a poke, to be filled with oil, dried and cooked meat, and edible roots and greens. An entry point the width of an arm was left and sealed with a wooden plug, allowing the women to dig inside for the food that sustained the family during the long winter months.

Needless to say, the construction of the storage sites— either a *siġluaq*, an ice cellar, or an aboveground cache on stilts—for this carefully preserved food was extremely important. Mice, voles, weasels, and larger animals like wolverines and bears and our own dogs were always foraging for food. We humans were just another part of the food chain, as the mosquitoes—which appeared by the billions during their short spurt of life in the spring and summer—reminded us every year.

When the brief summer ended and the days began to grow cold, we all moved from our tents on the beach to a sod house carved out of the earth. We could have built log homes, since logs were plentiful around Ikkattuq. But the *ivrulik* has been the home of the Iñupiat for a good ten thousand years, and we continued to build them in part because we loved the smell of the tundra from which they are made. It was, after all, the source of much of our livelihood, and its berries, roots, alders, spruce, grass, and willows all had made an indelible imprint on generations of Iñupiaq people.

The *ivrulik* was a simple structure—essentially a mound of earth fashioned into human living quarters—and it was completely appropriate to the frigid nine-month winters of my homeland. It took just a week or two to build. It was made of natural materials we could find in plentiful quantities all around us. It was inexpensive. And perhaps most important, it was warm. We had to build a new one every few years, in part because over time the old *ivrulik* became unsanitary, and in part because during the winter mice constantly drilled their way inside in search of warmth and food; eventually all those tiny holes in the walls made the interior of the *ivrulik* less warm.

Here's how we built it. We started with spruce logs for the center posts and corners, then added smaller split trees along the sides and on the roof. After this frame was in place, no taller than six feet at the highest point, we cut out large cubes of earth for the walls, leaving a single rectangular space for a window that would later be covered with beluga gut skin, which was translucent and allowed some light to shine in. We found tundra that was mossy, soft, and deep and cut it into long carpetlike strips for the roof, then added more sod for protection against wind and rain and cold. The floor of the *ivrulik* was dirt, but we covered it with willow branches, which gradually got trampled flat by our mukluks and boots. The entire structure encompassed less than 350 square feet. Anything larger than that would have been too hard to heat.

In earlier times, there was a small underground tunnel for the entrance, with places for food storage along the walls. That style of construction kept cold air from seeping into the living space as people came and went, and may also have served a protective function, since any would-be intruder had to crawl to get inside, making it easy to prevent his entrance. In a more modern *ivrulik*, the tunnel was replaced with a *qanitchaq*, a storm shed made of earth, timber, or an old tent, which provided considerably more storage for food and equipment. Another key feature of the *ivrulik* was the *qiŋak*, or "nose"—a hole in the sod roof, fitted with a short hollow log, which allowed the structure to breathe. Through it, stale air passed out and fresh air wafted in.

We had no real furniture. Beds consisted of willow branches piled a few inches deep along the walls. The piles were just wide enough for a body, and were held in place by logs, which separated the peripheral sleeping area from the rest of the floor. Each willow bed was covered with a *qaatchiaq*—a mattress made of caribou skin. Sleeping bags or blankets went on top of the *qaatchiaq*.

For almost every other purpose, we used Blazo boxes. Blazo was a brand of gasoline that was shipped to Kotzebue from Seattle. Two five-gallon cans came in a wooden crate to protect the Blazo on its three-thousand-mile journey. The wood of the crates was light, dry, and strong enough for endless uses. We turned them into cupboards, toolboxes, grub boxes, chairs, boat seats, dressers, and, when necessary, kindling. Our dining table was a Blazo box cut in two. At mealtime, we would place it in the center of the floor and put the food on it and sit to eat on our haunches, on logs, on five-gallon cans—or on more Blazo boxes. After each meal, we put the makeshift table away.

Next to the entry of the *ivrulik* we stacked our rifles and shotguns in case ptarmigan, ducks, or caribou showed up. In the opposite corner sat our homemade stove, which was actually a forty-two-gallon fuel drum with a burner on top and an oven cut out in the bottom. Sometimes, during the day, the stove would glow red with the heat. We didn't have to keep the fire going all night; the heat from our bodies was enough to keep the space livable—except in the dead of night, when going to the bathroom was always a production.

We all slept on the floor, and there was generally little open space. So if you woke with a need, first you would try to find a flashlight, if there was one. Then you would try to avoid stepping on someone as you made your way outside, where it might be ten or twenty degrees below zero with a howling wind. One winter, we built a multiroom *anaġvik* (loosely translated: a place to defecate) out of a big snowbank. To me, as a young boy, it seemed palatial, and I enjoyed walking from room to room examining the little brown piles of *anaq* frozen in odd configurations.

But most of the time, the bathroom arrangements were far more primitive. One awful experience of mine has become a part of family lore. We had just returned to camp from a dog-team trip to Kotzebue, a trip that took between six and eight hours, depending on conditions and the load. In town, we had stocked up on bubble gum, hard candy, and candy bars, and I managed to get a major stomachache from eating too many of the goodies. They gave me *iliktaq*—a diarrhea remedy made of roasted flour—but it didn't work.

In the dead of night, I awoke in desperate straits. There was little light, I was disoriented, and I couldn't find the five-gallon can we used as an indoor potty. I ran about in vain, squirting uncontrollably. Finally I could hold it no longer and just squatted. In the morning, the mess was apparent to everyone, but no one was angry with me, and it has been a family joke ever since that I had missed the head of my sleeping brother Umiivik—James—by just a few inches.

Particularly out in the bush, dogs had a special place in our lives. It always seemed to me like the perfect deal, one that went back to well before we crossed the Bering land bridge from Siberia to North America ten or twelve thousand years ago: we kept them alive and they kept us alive.

In the world of the Iñupiat, vast distances had to be covered in the normal course of living, and there were three ways to do it: you walked, boated, or traveled by dog team. Since most of our year was winter, when walking and boating were largely out of the question, dogs were critical in virtually all aspects of life: moving the family from campsite to campsite, getting us to traplines or hunting grounds, hauling food and fuel to our homes. In the winter, they pulled sleds; in the summer, they carried loads of caribou meat across the difficult muskeg and tussocks using a *nakmauti*—a specially made pack of sealskin or canvas with pouches on the sides that fitted over the dog's back.

Sometimes in my youth we had as few as seven dogs, sometimes as many as fifteen. Dogs and people ate the same foods—dried fish, seal meat, blubber, caribou, whale, walrus, salmon. Sometimes, when supplies were short, we had to make a choice between saving them or us. It was not an easy choice, since we needed the dogs to survive. And when times were really tough, the dogs themselves might become the meal. Fortunately, we never reached the point in our family when we had to eat our dogs, although I have been hungry enough to do so.

As soon as I was big enough to harness the dogs, I would be outside helping to load the sled and hitch the team in the right order. The dogs would be barking and carrying on, leaping about, eager to do what they were born to do—to pull. We used all kinds of combinations to try to get the best pull possible on the loaded sleds, switching the dogs around until we got it right. Unlike the Iñuit Greenlanders, who arrange the dogs in a fan-shaped formation, we hitched them in a series of pairs. Some dogs were very strong and we used them at the "wheel" next to the sled—a dangerous position, since the sled occasionally ran into and over them. If a dog was particularly troublesome, we would put it at the wheel as punishment.

Having a brilliant lead dog was a tremendous asset. Your team helped establish your identity as a successful person in the Iñupiaq world, and having your leader's litter in demand was a great compliment. More important, your leader could mean the difference between life and death, helping you find your way home in a blinding storm, leading you around the thin ice, and stopping the team if you somehow fell off the runners.

Dogs reflected much about the character of their owners. People controlled them through love or through fear or through a combination of both. Some men were mean and quick with the whip, and on occasion I saw dogs with chains so tight that their necks bled. Other masters used words and whistles—calling the dogs by their names and encouraging them when the going was tough. We always treated our dogs well. If a dog did a particularly good job at whatever task was required, it would get an extra portion of food at the end of the day. If a dog caused a big ruckus, it might go to bed hungry and get a beating. I've never studied it, but I suspect there is a correlation between how a man raises his dogs and how he treats his children.

We didn't have the luxury of keeping dogs that didn't carry their load. When a dog's productive days were over, no matter how much you might love it, you had to help him quickly move on into the other world. As a young boy, I once had the duty of shooting a dog I liked because her useful life had passed. I remember walking that dog to the dump. I just knew she was aware this was her last mile. She stood there, waiting for me to shoot her with the .30-30. I almost couldn't do it. But I did.

I remember only one exception to the usual rules of canine-human relations. When I was five or six years old, we had a litter. One of the puppies, barely able to walk, took to waddling under the stove at night to get warm. There were ashes and soot under there, and one morning when he crawled out, covered with crud, I said to Naungaġiaq: "We should name him Puya." *Puya* was our word for "dirty" or "seal-oil residue."

So Puya he became. Perhaps because I grew attached to him, he also became the only dog we ever allowed to live with us like a member of the family. He had free rein to come and go and slept on the floor along with the rest of us at night, usually next to me.

Puya grew to be a large dog with a rather sad expression but a friendly disposition; he only rarely got into a fight. I can't recall Puya's ever having to don a harness to earn his keep as every other dog had to do. He didn't have to curl up in the snow when the temperature was thirty or forty below zero and the wind was blowing; he didn't face the prospect of falling through the ice in the fall or pulling the sled through the deep drifts after a snowfall in the winter. He had a good life and lived to a ripe old age. He died just a few weeks before I returned home from high school. He had been there to keep me company when I was asleep on the floor. He had played with me on the beaches and in the snowdrifts when we were at camp and I had no human playmates. I have only one photograph of Puya and me, taken one summer day. But his spirit is still with me in spite of all the years I've traveled away from home.

One fall, we were living at Ikkattuq and the water rose so quickly that we had to abandon our sod house. We have a word for what happened—*ulit*, which means the earth had turned inside out. For days there had been heavy rains in the mountains, saturating the land, and gradually all the rivers grew swollen and angry. At the same time, a west wind started blowing from offshore, pushing even more water from Kotzebue Sound up into the inlets. When we went to bed one evening, we thought everything would be all right. But in the middle of the night we awoke to find that the water was at our door.

In a scramble, we gathered everything and ran to higher ground about a half mile away. We pitched tents and stayed there until the water receded, and the older family members began work on a new *ivrulik* upriver at Qimikpuk, a site at the foot of some low hills and at a bend in the river. Sometimes, when the air is right and the wind calm, you can hear sounds over a great distance, and one of my vivid memories from that fall is the sound of ice skates in the crisp air, as my older brothers returned at dusk from building that new *ivrulik*. They would come back tired, cold, and ready for a big hot meal: caribou stew, sourdough bread, seal oil with dried fish, and plenty of coffee or tea, topped off with a dessert of salmonberries or *qayusaaq*, cooked cranberries. We also enjoyed foods from Outside, as we had ever since trade began with the Siberians in the 1700s and we started using processed products—tea, sugar, coffee, and tobacco, to name

a few—that would ruin our health. And the whalers introduced us to pilot bread (*qaqqulaaq*), which to this day I must
have with my tea, spread with peanut butter and strawberry
jam.

It was not long before we were ready to move into the
new sod house. My mother Naunġaġiaq led me and my sister
inland. I was carrying a puppy. We had to walk because the
other family members needed the dog teams to carry heavy
household items. So naturally, I was cold and exhausted by
the time we reached a bend in the river. As we trudged
along, Anugaq (Benny), a cousin who had joined our family
shortly before Saigulik and I arrived, appeared behind us
with a sled loaded with goods. We were thrilled to catch a
ride. I asked how far we had to go.

"It's way up there," said Benny. I looked up to see a range
of hills not too far off—but beyond them, looming in the distance, a dark blue mountain. That was where Benny was
pointing.

I was crestfallen.

Just then I smelled the wonderful odor of burning spruce.
Benny had been teasing me. Our new house was just around
the bend, hidden in the trees. It was one of the happiest moments of my young life.

At Qimikpuk, we trapped and hunted fur-bearing animals.
Each animal had its own trails and its particular ways of living, and we hunted them accordingly, scouting out their
habitat and using bait appropriate to their species and traps
appropriate for their size. We caught rabbits—and sometimes
ptarmigan as well—with wire snares. For other creatures, we
had steel traps, ranging from small ones for muskrats to giant ones for wolves and bears.

I remember one spring when we caught about four hundred muskrats. At that time, a large trapped muskrat brought in three dollars, a dollar more than one that had been shot, as the traders didn't like bullet holes in the skin. Our trapping success that year enabled us, for the first time, to buy an outboard motor. That 5-horsepower Johnson engine made it seem as if we were flying, and it helped our livelihood immeasurably, allowing us to hunt and fish more widely and with considerably greater success.

We also trapped lynx, land otter, fox, ermine, and wolverine. These pelts were prized by our own people for clothing and also brought good prices in the trading posts so that we could buy necessities such as tea, bacon, potatoes, ammunition, cloth, needles, matches, flour, and sunglasses.

Eventually the family decided to move back to the coast. Working together, we built a raft of spruce logs and—at a snail's pace—towed the raft down the Little Noatak to the spot where we had escaped the flood. There we built the third *ivrulik* of my childhood—the only one I actually helped to construct. By this time I was strong enough to lift the large cubes of earth and carry them to the frame. I also could help roll the larger pieces of sod, moss, and intertwined roots of berries and plants we used on the roof.

Those years at Ikkattuq, Qimikpak, and other places we lived along the shores of Kotzebue Sound and the Noatak River imprinted on me the deepest lessons of the life our people had lived since time immemorial. We knew that the forces of nature demanded respect. We knew that waste was an archenemy. We knew that cooperative effort was imperative—only by working together could we survive.

4

Aachıkkaŋ! I'm Scared!

When I was six and we were out in camp, the family shared some *utniq*, a delicacy much prized for its pungency. *Utniq* is made from the flippers of walrus or bearded seal, or *ugruk*, the source of the treat we ate. The flippers are prepared with extreme care, first immersed in the animal's blubber, then encased in the seal's own skin, turned inside out. Then the sealskin package is stored in a cool, dry spot for several months or even a year, depending on the conditions. Over time, the flipper inside it essentially ferments—becomes pickled—and it is a treat much enjoyed, especially among our elders.

What my family could not see or smell that fateful day was that the flipper we were consuming was teeming with botulism. Apparently the careful preparation necessary had been somehow bungled, and in short order we were all stricken ill. My brother Aġnaġaq—hallucinating from his share of the flipper—climbed into the *qayaq* and paddled the ten miles back to Kotzebue and staggered to the Native Service Hospital, where they saved his life by pumping his stomach and dosing him with alcohol. Most of our family made it, but Aġnaġaq's wife Evelyn didn't and neither did the baby she was carrying. Aqpayuk, my adopted father, also died.

The death of Aqpayuk—still in his early fifties—was a devastating blow from which we never really recovered. It was a profound loss: the head of the family, and a man of such strength and great hunting skills. I've often thought that had he survived, Aqpayuk might have been able to prevent the alcohol from affecting so many of us, and I know I would have benefited mightily from his tremendous knowledge about our language and culture.

Naunġaġiaq, like many Arctic women who lost their husbands, never remarried. She simply carried on as she always had with the morning-to-night labor it took to keep the family fed, housed, and clothed without benefit of any modern conveniences. And her cheerful disposition never deserted her. She seemed to have the strength and persistence to face anything. When their parents could not care for them, she took in her children's children and her great-nieces and -nephews. When alcoholism and illness struck members of her family, she cared for them as best she could.

After my father's death, the vacuum of family leadership was filled by Umiivik, James Hensley, Naunġaġiaq and Aqpayuk's fourth child. Umiivik had never married. He'd had little schooling, and I can't remember him ever reading anything. And like many of our young men, he had bouts with alcohol. But he loved the country, which he may have seen as an antidote to the temptations of town, and after Aqpayuk died, Umiivik took me under his wing so that I could learn the ropes of survival out on the tundra. We boated together, hunted ducks and muskrat, gathered seagull eggs, and set nets under the ice for sheefish. I enjoyed being his little right-hand man. I generally felt inadequate to almost all the tasks, but I think he appreciated my energy and enthusiasm.

Although I didn't know it as a child, I was essentially an apprentice. Every task I performed for the family, every time I was invited to go somewhere with one of my older relatives, I was, in fact, learning how to survive. As soon as I was old enough to work the pump that pressurized the portable Primus stove, I was assigned a special morning duty. I was expected to get up in the near dark on a cold winter day, and in the dim light from the gut-skin window of the sod house, I would find my way to the corner, pump the stove, strike a wooden match, and hope that I had enough air in the cylinder so that there would be a nice short blue flame. I would chop up some ice with the pick and put it in the coffeepot to melt and boil. Once it boiled, I would put four or five handfuls of coffee—it was almost always Hills Brothers—into the water, let it boil for a few minutes, then add a dash of cold water to settle the grounds. Then I served the coffee to Umiivik, Naunġaġiaq, and whoever else was awake and needed a jolt to get them warm and ready to face the day. The house was so small that even that little Primus stove gave off enough heat to kill the chill.

On an ordinary day at camp, the men would usually eat breakfast first, before the women and children. The *ivrulik* was the domain of women and girls during the day, and men and boys were expected to get out quickly to do whatever was necessary to maintain life out in the country. The fastest way for a young boy to ruin his reputation was to spend too much time in the *ivrulik* when there was work to do outside. If you spent too much time inside, someone might say, "You will make somebody a good wife!"

If members of the family were headed off on a trip—checking a trapline, going ice fishing, or hunting caribou, for instance—the women would prepare a snack. Usually that meant a thermos of coffee or tea, some sourdough or pilot bread, dried caribou or whitefish, and a container of seal oil with bite-size bits of seal meat and dried fish, or maybe some little rectangles of cooked beluga skin—*maktak*. If it was a longer trip, the men would bring a small tent, utensils, a pot, a coffeepot, and maybe an onion or two and some potatoes, plus the trusty Primus stove and some matches. You would never leave without your favorite knife, a saw or an ax, a rifle, shotgun, telescope, and compass.

For those staying behind, there was plenty to be done: chopping wood, collecting ice that could be melted for drinking water, washing clothes, checking rabbit or ptarmigan snares, making fishing nets out of twine, cleaning rifles and any number of other tasks. This was no country for lazy-bones.

When we went to bed at night, someone would turn off the Coleman lamp. It took a minute or two for the mantle to dim, and then the interior of the *ivrulik* would be completely black. We were just inches from each other; usually it didn't take long for the snoring to start. I would lie there thinking about my friends down in Kotzebue, which seemed a million miles away, or wondering when I might get a larger rifle or a shotgun of my own, or dreaming of the time when I would be allowed to go on a caribou hunt. Now and then I stayed up and waited for the *aviŋaurat*—the mice. Every winter, they found their way into the *ivrulik* in search of warmth and sustenance, and after the humans stopped moving, they'd come out to search for food. When I heard scraping noises, I'd flick on a flashlight and, armed with a small slingshot, fire away at the little moving targets. Although it never occurred to me at the time—this was just a boy's idea of fun!—it was one of the many ways I was learning the hunting skills I would need to survive, and would pass on to my own children when the time came.

As I grew bigger, I began helping one of our relatives, Jackson Beaver, who was a hunchback. He was very smart but not very strong, so he invited me to boat with him and accompany him on forays with the dog team.

I learned a lot. One of the most important lessons involved *piyaquq*, which, loosely translated, is a tendency to be accident-prone. This is not a trait to have in a hunting environment. If you have it, others will avoid you in the wild: it is simply too dangerous to be out there with you.

I learned this indelibly one fall day when I was about ten. Jackson Beaver invited me to go upriver, a journey of several hours, to set some hooks for ling cod. Because of his disability, he couldn't dig the holes in the ice. So I took the *tuuq*, an implement with a sharp point on a fairly heavy shaft, and started to dig the first of the holes. Just as I broke through the ice, the *tuuq* slipped through my hands and went straight to the bottom of the river. That ended our work for the day. Jackson just looked at me.

He didn't have to utter a word. I was never so thoroughly embarrassed. Thankfully, that incident did not foreshadow any continuing tendency toward *piyaquq* on my part, and I continued to be a helpful hunting companion.

One overcast and snowy day, after consuming my share of the sourdough pancakes, I decided to grab my family's .22 rifle and walk inland to search for ptarmigan—*aqargit*. The birds were a staple of our diet in the winter and a joy to hunt because of their unusual calls—an unmistakable *qa-wer*, *qa-wer, qup, qup, qup.* They were always difficult to see because in the summer they were the color of the tundra and in the winter they turned snowy white. Sometimes in the winter they would fly in huge flocks, in which case one shotgun shell could net you quite a number. Other times, they were few and far between, and you'd have to pick them off one at a time. Sometimes I set snares for them along their little trails.

On that particular day, I knew the ptarmigan would be relatively easy to approach. On clear days, it seemed they could hear your footsteps a quarter mile away and they would fly off before you could get near enough to even fire a shot. But this day was perfect for ptarmigan hunting. The falling snow and clouds would muffle sound, including the noise of footsteps and shots. And the snow wasn't very deep, which meant it was fairly easy to walk along the trails.

I saw a flock of about twenty land just beyond a knoll and decided that I would crawl to the top and let them have it as they cackled around, unaware of my presence. But as I got near the top of the knoll, I suddenly saw something I did not expect. Twenty yards away was a large, ghostly apparition staring at me intently with enormous yellow eyes. *Aachikkaŋ!* (*I'm scared!*) It was a huge *ukpik*, a snowy owl, looking mean and fierce and entirely unafraid of this pipsqueak with a dainty little rifle in his hand.

I remembered one of my brothers shooting at an *ukpik* like that once—using a much bigger rifle. I dropped down onto one knee and fired. The *ukpik* leapt into the air, spreading its terrifying wings—maybe as great as four feet across—and soared down toward the ptarmigan, which scattered frantically in its path. Then it hit the snow-covered ground.

I tore down the hill, my heart pounding. I was terrified to approach the *ukpik*. What if it was only stunned or slightly wounded? It might attack me with its huge, sharp talons and beak. I took out my pocketknife and cut a limb from an alder tree. Gingerly, I used it to poke the huge *ukpik*. It didn't move. Finally, feeling proud as hell, I grabbed it by one wing tip and started walking back to our sod house. Every once in a while, the owl fell into one of my deep footprints in the snow, and just for a moment I would be badly startled, thinking it had come to life.

I dragged the *ukpik* home. Everyone was proud of me. Nauṅaġiaq plucked it, took off the wings and feet, and made a stew. We used the wings for a broom and made the feet into a toy, tying the ends of the foot muscles with sinew so that we could make those impressive talons open and close almost as they had in life.

To those from the outside world, we might have seemed destitute, but despite the loss of Aqpayuk, the family labored on, and it was a good life—if your health permitted it to be. Sadly, we were susceptible to every strange germ that came our way, and without medicines or clinics, illnesses that should never have claimed us often did. Thus Aqpayuk and Evelyn were poisoned by botulism. Ruby died from the flu, and my sister Saigulik—Frances—died in her twenties of a liver disease she may have caught from food contaminated by mice. Other family members died, one by one, of a host of cancers and other diseases.

Yet every day was an adventure, and we all took pleasure in the *anigniq*—the breath of life. No one ever feared death, although many came close to it. We greeted each morning with great expectations. What would the weather be like? Might some ptarmigans be roosting on the *ivrulik*—could we be lucky enough to catch a few so easily and quickly? Would there be anything in the fox trap? Was it time to check the sheefish net again? Should someone take the dog team and pick up a load of spruce? Was it time for a trip to town to stock up on supplies?

Umiivik was the eldest, and if anyone wanted to take the dogs, he would have to agree. He was more sober and planned more carefully than his younger brothers. Aaron and Isaac would go through their cartons of Camels and Lucky Strikes too fast after the fall freeze-up and by December would begin to tear up the place looking for the butts they had carelessly discarded when they had plenty of cigarettes left—and then, finally, they would suggest to Umiivik that it was time to go to town. That was always an issue because there were so many temptations down in Kotzebue. Who would take care of the dogs if Aaron and Isaac ran into a party or someone started a card game or one of the brothers got to winning down at Pete's pool hall? How could we be sure they would spend what money we had on what we actually needed? More often than not, Umiivik would decide to accompany his brothers on these trips so that he could supervise. Naunġaġiaq, Saigulik, and I would hold the fort during their absence.

There were some nights when the moon was full and the sky was clear and you could almost read under the starlit sky, with not a whiff of wind in the air. The snow would crunch loudly underfoot when one of us headed out to the cache to dig into the barrel of cranberries or to fetch some dried meat and seal oil. Other times the wind would howl, sending the snow swirling so thickly that it was impossible to see more than a few feet ahead. Those storms could last for days on end, and all we could do was hunker down and entertain ourselves with chores and games—and storytelling.

Naunġaġiaq told stories that I remember to this day. One

involved an elderly woman and her grandson who lived near the coast. Walking along the beach, the grandson found a seal—*natchiq*—and ate it. He returned home and warmed himself by the fire, bringing no food for his grandmother. Another day, he went out and came upon a bearded seal—*ugruk*. Again, he ate it and headed home with nothing to offer his grandmother. Finally he caught a whale—*aġviq*. Once more, he had a huge feast and returned with not a scrap for his grandmother. He sidled up to the stove to get warm, but got too close and suddenly there was a gigantic explosion. He disappeared. In his place were all the animals he had eaten, brought back to life. His grandmother survived by jumping aboard a huge wooden plate and paddling away, using a wooden spoon.

Another story took place in Kotzebue, up near the lagoon, where a family—including a mother with a baby still being suckled—lived in tents for the summer. One morning the family woke to find that overnight the baby's mouth had grown huge and had filled with teeth, and that it had eaten most of the mother. The family made a dash toward the village to get away from the baby, which crawled after them with amazing speed. They crossed the creek on a log, making it to safety. But *ataata*—grandfather—had forgotten his favorite jade knife and had to go back. He crossed the creek, made it to the tent, and grabbed the knife just as the baby came after him, snapping its huge jaws and teeth. As fast as he could, *ataata* ran to the creek, almost falling into the water as he scrambled across the log. Just as he stepped onto the opposite bank, the baby reached the log—and *ataata*, using all his strength, pulled the log toward him. The saber-toothed baby fell into the creek and drowned.

To this day, my hair stands on end when I walk along that creek up by Kotzebue's lagoon.

5

Kigutiŋu: Toothache

Before we were inundated with sugar, soft drinks, candy, coffee, tea, and cigarettes, our people had terrific teeth. We had to. Teeth were absolutely critical to Iñupiaq life as it was lived in the old days.

For one thing, consider our food—hunted, caught, or gathered, at the appropriate time of the year, from the sea, the air, and the land. Like people everywhere before refrigerators and freezers became common, we had to preserve it so that we could keep our families going when game was scarce. That meant stripping the meat from caribou, moose, reindeer, seals, walruses, whales, and whatever else we trapped or shot, harpooned or hooked, then drying it on racks in the air and sun before storing it, usually in seal oil. In the winter, we also froze food—game as well as sheefish, trout, arctic char, and tomcod—to preserve it. But both drying and freezing tended to make the food tough, difficult to chew. That was especially true of *maktak,* the whale-skin delicacy that is enjoyed by all Iñupiat to this day. It is virtually impossible to eat *maktak* unless you have good teeth.

And we needed good teeth for more than eating. Teeth served men and women alike as another tool, just as useful and essential as the harpoons, snares, rifles, knives, and other items necessary for our existence. Iñupiat women, for example, used their teeth to crimp dried sealskins to make soles for footgear—mukluks. They would dampen the skins, cut them to a size a bit larger than the feet they would protect, then bite carefully and evenly around them—trying to make each crimp identical to its neighbor—and thus turn the flat skin into a foot-shaped container. Mothers taught their daughters this art, along with the sewing skills—using dried sinews from caribou legs, "thread" that the women's teeth had also helped to prepare—needed to finish the mukluks. Depending on the size of her family, a woman might have to make ten or more pairs of mukluks a year. So if she learned at her mother's side as a girl and lived to be fifty-five, she could easily make four hundred pairs or more during her lifetime. By the time my mother Nauṅaġiaq reached middle age, her teeth were pretty much worn down to her gums from all that work.

So teeth, for us, were extremely important. And before civilization brought us all the products that threatened their health, we had no need for the raft of commercial products that enhance dental hygiene, although we occasionally used a sharp stick or a bit of sinew to dislodge some stubborn bit of food.

By the time I was growing up, we needed those hygienic products—yet we knew virtually nothing about them. We had no running water, and few families could afford amenities like toothpaste. I never had a toothbrush as a child, and there wasn't a dentist within hundreds of miles. When dental floss first showed up on the shelves of Kotzebue's stores, it was hugely popular—but not, it turned out, for cleaning teeth. The Iñupiat women quickly discovered that floss was strong, tough, and slippery smooth, easily drawn through tough hides with a needle, and began using it as a substitute for caribou sinews in sewing mukluks!

Meanwhile, the traders sold us whatever we wanted and could pay for, and candy bars were always right there at eye level when we wandered into the stores. So not surprisingly, by the time I was ten my teeth were a mess. My smile revealed two front teeth riddled with holes. Several of my molars were so rotten that the nerves were nearly exposed. The pain grew worse and worse. Every time I took a bite of ptarmigan, or even something as soft as cooked whitefish, I felt as if someone inside my mouth was jabbing my gums with a tiny branding iron. I tried as hard as I could not to show how much I was suffering. After all, our people expected even an eight-year-old to be stoic and uncomplaining, and I was ten.

But finally that fall, when our family was out in the bush, my jaw began to swell. The ache became sharper, steady and constant. At night, I lay in the caribou skin sleeping bag on my bed of willows and cried, as quietly as I could. The family could not help noticing, but there was little they could do. There we were, ten miles from Kotzebue. The weather was just reaching freezing temperatures, and the ice was too thin for walking or skating and too thick to get through with a boat. I was stuck until the ice firmed up.

My brother Niŋaugaġraq—Aaron—was about ten years older than me, and we did a lot of hunting and net-setting together. One day he approached the subject directly.

"Iġġiaġruk, you want me to try being Dr. Rabeau?" he asked, referring to Stuart Rabeau, the physician at the Alaska

Native Hospital in Kotzebue who served, all by himself, a region larger than the state of Indiana.

"What you gonna try?" I asked.

Aaron reached into his pocket and pulled out a small, half-empty can of Copenhagen chewing tobacco, a treasured luxury. He placed a pinch of the stuff on each side of my lower jaw. And for a while, it worked. The pain abated a little—until suddenly I got woozy from the blast of nicotine in my thin body, a bit like getting an instant hangover. It seemed to me that Aaron's cure, kind and generous as his gesture had been, was even worse than the ailment. I continued to suffer, and as the days passed, my normally narrow face grew round with abscesses.

Fortunately, once it begins to freeze in Alaska, it can get very cold very fast. One night, the temperature dropped to twenty below zero, and the next day Aaron and Nauṅaġiaq decided that he and I should try to get to Kotzebue by dog team to get me some help.

Since this was the first such trip of the season, the dogs went crazy with excitement, leaping and jerking at their chains. Aaron and I hitched seven of them to our eight-foot sled and kept the load as light as possible. Aaron did bring some rope, a .22-caliber rifle, and his *tuuq*, to test the thickness of the ice along the way. He also packed a knapsack with dried whitefish and crackers.

"*Kiikka!* Let's go!" he yelled. And off we went.

No snow had fallen yet to provide traction for the dogs, and we were traveling over bare, slippery ice. Even so, since we had no load to speak of, the team had little trouble pulling the sled. We headed toward Pipe Spit, a half-mile gravel finger that juts, like the spit on which Kotzebue lies, off the Baldwin Peninsula. Pipe Spit is about three miles east of Ikkattuq across Hotham Inlet—Kobuk Lake, as we call it.

If we could reach it, we planned to follow the shoreline to Kotzebue. That was the long way around—about ten miles farther than the ten-mile direct course across Kotzebue Sound—but we couldn't trust the ice.

As we neared Pipe Spit, we could see smoke curling from the Satterlees' cabin, and knew that if we made it, we'd soon be treated to hot tea and good company. But there was a hidden danger between our sled and that neighborly haven. Two big rivers, the Kobuk and the Selawik, empty into Kobuk Lake. All that water flows fast and deep just off Pipe Spit's shore, and the force of the current keeps the ice from freezing as quickly and solidly as it does in quieter, shallower waters. Every now and then Aaron would use his *tuuq* to check the ice. And it was obvious that it was thin—growing even thinner as we got closer to Pipe Spit. We could see the dark water rushing beneath the sled as we glided along.

About halfway across the inlet, Tapit, one of our dogs, suddenly seemed to fall apart. At first she ran awkwardly. Then she came down on her hind legs and couldn't even walk properly. Her spine must have been injured during the journey over the slick ice. There were no veterinarians in all of western and northern Alaska in those days; I don't think we even knew such a profession existed. So Aaron did what had to be done. He shot Tapit to end her misery. We left her on the ice and kept moving.

As we slid along, we could hear the ice begin to crack. Aaron called out "Whoa!" to the dogs, and we glided to a stop. He started walking ahead of the team. He drove the *tuuq* into the ice, and this time it went right through. He scrambled back to the sled and we decided to head a bit farther south, where the current might not be so fast and the ice might be thicker, before turning back toward Pipe Spit. When Aaron tested the ice again, the *tuuq* didn't go all the way through. Ever so carefully, we crept forward, finally making it to the gravel beach on the spit's south end. The Satterlees had been watching our entire ordeal, and were ready with tea and food and convivial conversation for a couple of hours before we headed for Kotzebue.

The next morning, Aaron walked me from our house in town to the hospital. I had been inside the building before, for various vaccinations. But this was an entirely new experience.

Dr. Stuart Rabeau was a big man. To me, he seemed like a giant. He had receding dark brown hair, was soft and blubbery, and there was almost always a huge cigar stuck in his mouth. In those days, as the only doctor in the hospital, he handled every imaginable medical problem. Most Iñupiat thought he was unfriendly and gruff. And most of us were positively afraid of Alice Connelly, the nurse who was always at his side. She was just as unpleasant as she looked— so unpleasant, in fact, that many years later, I was all but certain that she had been the model for the disagreeable Nurse Ratched in *One Flew Over the Cuckoo's Nest*.

Dr. Rabeau greeted me kindly enough. "Willie, what can I do for you?" he asked. I told him that I needed to have my teeth pulled. He looked inside my mouth for a few seconds and whistled. Then he asked Miss Connelly to prepare some Novocain.

I almost fainted when I saw the length of the needle. Dr. Rabeau shot both sides of my jaw full of the painkiller, and I pushed back into the chair as deep as I could get until he pulled out the needle.

After waiting a few minutes, Dr. Rabeau began poking around inside my mouth with his finger. Then he grabbed a gleaming pair of pliers and started to pull one of my rotten molars. I could feel what he was doing and jerked away, telling Dr. Rabeau that it hurt. He asked Miss Connelly to hold my head. She grabbed it as hard as she could and Dr. Rabeau once again began pulling. I could hear the molar's root crack free and feel the blood spurt into my mouth, and I screamed. The Novocain had not taken effect.

But by now both doctor and nurse were determined to finish the business. They moved in on the other side of my jaw, and before I knew it, they had yanked out another molar. I cried from the pain. They dabbed out the blood and sent me home to our cold little house, weak-kneed and sniffling. I curled up inside and slept until Aaron returned and we could head back to Ikkattuq.

Four long years later, I finally made it to a real dentist, Dr. Robert Lathrop, who came to Kotzebue from Barrow by dog team with his wife Petey. He drilled and filled for weeks, it seemed, and was able to save enough of my teeth so that later, dentists could hang something man-made onto the stumps.

But I saw Dr. Rabeau several more times during my youth. And we had an unexpected reunion when I was attending George Washington University in Washington, D.C. One evening, I was lured out of my dorm room by an American Indian woman I had met during a summer job at the Bureau of Indian Affairs. We went to a dark rock-and-roll joint in town, where a drunken soldier started harassing my companions. I intervened, and later in the evening he hit me from the side, smashing my glasses into my right eye. He was arrested. I ended up in an emergency room having small shards of glass pulled from my eye. One of the doctors said I needed surgery within twenty-four hours or I would probably lose my sight.

I had heard that Dr. Rabeau, that same Stuart Rabeau who

had been in Kotzebue, was now the head of the Indian Health Service for the entire United States, so I called him up. "Willie, again, what can I do for you?" he asked. I explained my problem, and he offered to set me up with one of his doctors. He sent me to a military hospital in Baltimore, where they saved my eye.

As for Aaron, my brother, who had delivered me from awful pain that faraway fall in Ikkattuq, he eventually lost all but one front tooth. He detested the notion of going to see a dentist and couldn't imagine himself wearing dentures. Considering the pain I endured with Dr. Rabeau and Miss Connelly, I think Aaron could have been just as effective as they were at pulling my molars, and I might have saved myself a lot of grief if I had taken him up on his original offer to play dentist. But thanks to him, more than half a century later— with my natural teeth intact—I can still eat dried fish, *quaq* (frozen fish or meat), and *maktak* (whale skin).

6

Qıtıktuaqtugut: We Play

If we survived, it was because we worked hard. But make no mistake: we also played hard. In spring, when the ice would thaw and eventually rot and begin its long journey down the rivers to Kotzebue Sound, then into the Arctic Ocean, we could not resist playing *mauliġauraq. Mauliq* means to accidentally fall through the ice.

We would play follow-the-leader across small pans of ice, flying over them before they sank. Usually the water wasn't too deep, so if someone fell in completely, the fall was merely embarrassing. But in town, the breakup of the ice was spectacular. The village was on a gravel spit, and the ice—four or five feet thick—was squeezed between the spit and the shoals a few hundred yards offshore. A huge mountain of the stuff would form on the north side of the spit. And if the mass of ice was moving nearby, our game was definitely dangerous, and potentially fatal. On occasion, one of us would end up marooned on a large ice pan heading out to sea, and someone with a boat would have to rescue him.

This was a game to us, but the skill, speed, and body control necessary to do it successfully were essential when hunting seals and whales. If, for instance, you had to move fast to make it across thin ice, you had to make your body as light as possible. This game was a good test of that ability.

To a degree, all the games we played also helped hone our survival skills. When the spring thaw flooded parts of the village, we built rafts out of fifty-gallon drums and paddled around. We made slingshots out of willows, leather, and rubber to hunt snipes and ducks. All that paddling and hunting were good preparation for more serious work. In the short summer months, I constructed miniature boats out of tin from gasoline cans and pulled them along the beach with a string and a pole. If you really wanted to be creative, you could build a fake outboard motor and add a small propeller that would twirl around when you pulled the boat. I loaded them up with appropriate cargo—rocks or marbles or pieces of wood—and ran along the beach, trying to avoid the dogs tied to the meat racks that were built along the shore in front of the homes. Later I learned to make miniature *qayaqs* out of driftwood and caribou skin. My friend Henry Driggs (named for an early missionary doctor) and I would soak the skins until the hair fell out and stretch the skin tightly on a small driftwood frame and let it dry. We sold them to the occasional tourist who came to town, then used the proceeds to buy candy bars or soft drinks and maybe an ice cream cone over at Archie Ferguson's Farthest North Restaurant.

Sometimes we played Norwegian, a game we must have learned from the Lapps who had been hired by the federal government in the 1890s to teach reindeer husbandry to our people. The game involved a bat and ball and two teams, one fielding and the other batting. The teams stood on lines thirty or forty yards apart. The pitcher stood right on the line of the batting team and lobbed a soft rubber ball a couple of feet into the air. The batter hit it, then had to run like hell to reach the other team's line without getting hit by the ball. If he made it, he also had to make it back to the home line to score. If he got hit by the ball, he was out. The sides would switch once someone caught a fly ball or the batting team made a certain number of runs.

The other summer games were hopscotch, seesaws, and swings. The seesaws and swings were usually homemade, the former from planks balanced on fifty-gallon drums, the latter from timber and rope. At school, there was a large swing. Two kids would stand on the wooden seat, facing one another, and push until they were swinging so high that they were darn near airborne. They would also climb the supports on opposite sides and launch themselves at the center pole, twirling around it when they grabbed hold. That took a little nerve.

My friends and I all knew that strength, endurance, speed, accuracy, control, and stamina were highly esteemed in our culture. Sight, strength, hearing, judgment, and memory were all essential to survival. We had no idea that our generation was the last that would depend on the strength and agility of both human beings and their dogs—that the snow machine and outboard motor were about to render these ancient methods obsolete.

So we gloried in the games. You were expected to be modest about your strength and stamina, but in the periodic contests we call *anaktaq*, you could show what you could do. By the time I was growing up, those contests were beginning to be held during holiday celebrations such as Christmas and the Fourth of July. Especially the Fourth of July! It was not one of our traditional festivities, but from the moment the missionaries introduced this holiday at the turn of the last century, our people took to it.

Fireworks were a failure, since by July it's bright as day all night long. But firecrackers—we had plenty of those—and the games themselves went on day and night: there were footraces, dog-team races, *qayaq* races, *maktak*-eating contests, blanket tosses, and tug-of-war. There were even "baby buggy" races. Iñupiat mothers traditionally carry babies in the back of their parkas, held upright by a *tupsi*, a strap that ties around the mother's waist. That enables the woman to walk, run, and do chores with the baby safe and warm all the while. In the baby-buggy race, the women carried their babies in traditional style while they ran thirty or forty yards to a finish line.

There was also a variety of contests designed to exhibit strength in fingers, wrists, arms, legs, necks, and ankles. Kicking, leaping, dexterity, and control all combined in these contests. Some involved walking on your knees while holding your feet, or bouncing on your knuckles or elbows and toes across the floor to see who could travel farthest. Others involved kneeling, facing an opponent, and pushing your foreheads together until one of you couldn't stand the pain.

I loved to high-kick and was considered one of the better kickers. In those days, we did it for fun and didn't attempt to keep score. The goal was to kick a dangling sealskin ball as high as possible in a number of variations—two-footed kick, one-legged kick, kicking with your belt hitched over your head and under your knees while you balanced on your hands, and kicking with one leg while holding your other foot with one hand and balancing on the other.

I think in part these games were a way for young women to determine which young men they might eventually pair up with. After all, someone who was apparently physically fit made a good catch in the days when it took real strength to be a provider. Also, you would be seen and your family connections would be noted, and you might be wearing some pretty mukluks or a fancy parka indicating that your family had substance.

The winners were awarded ribbons and a small cash prize. The official would call the winner's name and he or she had to walk up in front and face the entire village. The official would then walk around the room and find a suitable person of the opposite sex to come up and pin the ribbon on the winner. Sometimes the person picked would make for an unlikely pairing—someone really homely for a really beautiful girl, for instance, or someone very fat for someone very skinny, or someone really tall for someone very short. There was always a huge roar—"*Hai! Hai!*"—from the crowd and the couple would blush and smile until they sat down.

Of course, not all of our playtime was spent in such physical exertions. To this day, one of my favorite pastimes is to *navraaqtuq*—dig for the old objects, the artifacts of my people's thousands of years on the site, that were always just a few inches under our feet. Sometimes after a huge wind the beach would unearth a piece of carved ivory or a flint harpoon or arrowheads and scrapers. If you were lucky, you might even find a piece of jade.

My people loved to play cards, even though I know the missionaries frowned on that activity, as they did on other "sins" like using lipstick and dancing. And we loved the movies. I have no idea when the first moving picture was shown in Kotzebue. But I recall quite clearly that the church my family attended, the Friends Church, was very much against movies; the Catholics, who showed them right in their church's large foyer, were clearly all going to go to hell.

I thought that if movies were the path to hell, it was going to be fun getting there—and I don't recall anyone trying to stop me. My friends and I took every opportunity to go to Archie Ferguson's Midnight Sun Theater, either getting some grownup to lend us twenty-five cents or, if necessary, sneaking in under someone else's parka. The movies took us to another world. We didn't know that it was just acting. To us, it was all real, stories of people and places that were completely alien to us. We gobbled it up.

Westerns were our favorites. Hopalong Cassidy. Tex Ritter. The gooey romance movies with their public displays of affection just embarrassed us. But we would really get into the wild western—the fancy horse tricks, the quick draws with the six-shooters, the brawling and falling off balconies. And the fierce Indians. For thousands of years, our people had had tense relations with the Itqiḷit who lived in the interior—tribal Indians whose culture and language were entirely different from ours. So we had little trouble assuming that the Indians were the villains. We took the bait Hollywood gave us and sided with the "good guys." We were unaware—entirely—of the fact that our own people had considerably more in common with the Indians than with their onscreen enemies. And having had a good dose of Christian religion, we were familiar with the word "Calvary." So at the end of the movies, when the pioneers—about to be obliterated by the screaming Indians on horseback—circled their covered wagons, we would shout, "Here comes the Calvary!" as the legions of soldiers on horseback appeared at the last minute. There was no one to tell us what the cavalry was, and to explain how different it was from the place where Jesus was crucified.

It was at the Midnight Sun Theater that I first saw someone being hypnotized. Elmer Ipalook took a little silver object, swung it slowly in front of someone's eyes, and then took complete command of the person. It was awesome. It was scary. I loved it.

No one actually spoke to me about sex until I was thirteen or so, around the time the hormones started really kicking in. Despite the fact that the missionaries had been doing their best to change the culture, in our part of the world there seemed to be a pretty open attitude about sex even in the late forties and early fifties.

Of course, we grew up surrounded by animals, which offered us an early understanding of reproduction. We knew how the breeding worked, since we frequently witnessed it among the dogs. And our homes were small, usually one room. In the dead of night, we could hear the heavy breathing of the adults as they went about their lovemaking. And when beds with springs became a part of our lives, I remember distinctly the squeaking that started slowly and built to a noisy climax. No one ever said anything about the racket. What was going on was pretty much left to our imaginations.

Since we spent so much time outdoors, both at work and at play, we had plenty of time to learn the facts of life on our own. In summer, for instance, it could become unbearably hot. We would walk a half mile to a lake that was connected to the lagoon by a small creek just deep enough for swimming. Because of taboos, we would not swim in the lagoon itself. It was said that a *nuiaqpalik*—a mermaidlike creature—lived there. But that fifty-yard creek was heaven, and we sometimes made two or three trips a day to cool off and have fun. The girls usually swam down next to the lake. But occasionally they would join us nearer the lagoon, where the water was clearer and deeper. We had no swimming suits, and some of us didn't even have shorts. We would cup our hands over our private parts and wade in. Once in a while the girls, too, would wade in naked. Needless to say, the boys were tantalized by their brazenness.

I remember one of the first occasions I became really conscious of a girl. We were out in the country at the mouth of the Little Noatak, dug into the beach, our shotguns handy, awaiting the arrival of spring ducks. I was with one of my classmates and his older adopted sister. She was beautiful and sensuous, with long black hair and teeth like white ivory. She told me about her travels Outside in the company of an older man. It became hard to concentrate on the ducks. My heart pounded away as she sat next to me, touching me occasionally as we kept our eyes on the horizon. This tense moment might have led somewhere had we not caught some mallards and in the excitement moved on home to *iġitchaq*—pluck—the catch.

It was different with a classmate of mine who had come to Kotzebue from a village up north. I think she and her older brother were stronger and tougher than us "city" kids. Somehow we ended up together when no one was home one evening, and it was obvious that she knew much more than I did about the facts of life. Her image is etched in my memory, and will be there until I am placed in the permafrost.

7

Umıaqpak: The North Star

There was one annual event in Kotzebue that was unlike any other. We all knew that it was coming, and we children, especially, could hardly stand the anticipation. One late-summer morning every year, we would wake up and see on the southern horizon the outline of a huge seagoing vessel: the *North Star*, out of Seattle, Washington, a place I only dimly understood was part of Outside.

The ship's primary function in the early days was to bring supplies for the schools that had been established in the villages by the U.S. government. But the *North Star* delivered far more than supplies. It brought the goods that the traders and businessmen sold in Alaska's coastal villages. It brought new people, and Iñupiaq families who hitched rides to visit relatives in distant towns. It brought sheer excitement of a kind we rarely experienced—and a tangible connection to the Outside world.

The coastal waters of the Arctic are shallow, since the sea

bottom was once part of the Bering land bridge, so the ship had to anchor eight miles or so off the beach. We could barely make out its shape on the horizon, but once we did, the waterfront exploded with activity as boats and barges joined in a frenetic effort to unload the Kotzebue cargo as quickly as possible so that the ship could sail on to supply other villages.

The block between Ferguson's Trading Post and Rotman's Store was the focal point. Night and day, fully laden barges would dock along the beach, secured by huge ropes to pilings that held up a shoreside warehouse. Archie Ferguson, the entrepreneur who owned the trading post, the air taxi service, the movie theater, a restaurant, a roadhouse, and a shipping company, oversaw the unloading. I can still see him in my mind's eye: short, pear-shaped, balding, sleeves rolled up, pants too short, wearing slip-on tan shoes, as he bounced about the area, supervising, singing, and whistling some off-key tune.

A conveyor contraption twenty yards long would be eased into place between a barge and the road along Kotzebue's beach. Once it was cranked up, the cases began to roll off the barge—tons of foodstuffs and general merchandise—and were carted off to warehouses for storage. They would be sold and used for an entire year until the *North Star* showed up again.

Helping unload the *North Star* was one of the few chances many local men had to earn some cash, and my brothers were always part of the action. Sometimes they came home completely white from carrying hundred-pound sacks of flour. The very next day, they might come home completely black from carrying sacks of coal. It was hard work, but it was a chance to pay the bills we had built up at the store during the winter, and to make some extra money so that we could afford essentials for the next year.

In those days before statehood, when Alaska was just a U.S. territory, it was legal for the businessmen to pay the workers with aluminum bingles—coinlike objects about the size of a fifty-cent piece, bearing a phrase such as "good for trade at Ferguson Stores, worth $1.00" or some other value. Archie Ferguson's bingles were good for trade only at Ferguson enterprises. You could buy some groceries at the trading post or go to his restaurant for a meal or to his Midnight Sun Theater for a movie or even fly to another village on his plane. But outside his little empire, those particular bingles were useless.

For families like mine, in which no one had the good fortune to hold a year-round job, this was a critical point in our economic cycle. We lived primarily off the land, hunting caribou in the fall, ptarmigan and rabbits in the winter, and sea mammals, geese, and other birds in the spring; catching salmon and a variety of other fish in the summer; gathering plants and berries whenever we could find them. In spring and summer, we tried to pay off what we owed with furs we had trapped and with labor, such as the *North Star* work.

In a good year, that gave us enough to buy things you couldn't find in the wild: coffee, sugar, beans, canned vegetables, oatmeal, canned milk, baking powder, and Sailor Boy pilot bread. If you could afford such supplies, you were well on your way to a decent winter. And if the fur trapping season had been really good, you might even buy a new oil-burning stove, a bed, a new shotgun, or even a small outboard motor.

In the villages upriver from the Arctic coast, the shelves

were usually pretty bare by the time the *North Star* arrived. Then, all of a sudden, they filled up with the things people had been craving for months: fresh eggs, fresh vegetables, and fresh fruit, as well as cookies, bacon, and a great deal of *naluaġmiutaq*—white man's food.

Needless to say, for children, the *North Star*'s arrival was an event that was hard to beat. And there was no shortage of places where we could enjoy the action as the ship disgorged its cargo. My friends and I would watch in fascination as the captain of the tug maneuvered the barge against the shore. We gaped at the mountains of merchandise. We listened to the engine of the conveyor contraption and watched its blasts of smoke curl up into the air. We delighted in the aroma of apples and oranges that filled the air. The captain and crew were very popular among the children. They always brought candy and gum, and after years of visits, they got to know us pretty well. I think they enjoyed watching us change as we grew up.

We envied my brothers, wishing that we, too, were big and strong enough to join the workforce. But most of all, we wanted to ride the tugboat out to the *North Star* itself. We imagined climbing aboard and exploring this monstrous vessel, able to carry such a vast array of goods. But you could visit the ship only if you knew someone who had an acquaintance among the *North Star*'s crew. Alas, I was just too shy to ask, and I never did get onboard.

In the fall, we saw the *North Star* once again in the midst of its trip south to Seattle from Barrow, the northernmost coastal outpost it had visited. The ship would stop in Kotzebue to pick up summer visitors: the families from Little Diomede Island—about halfway between Alaska and Siberia in the Bering Strait—who came to Kotzebue every summer in large *umiat*, skin boats, and set up tents along the shore.

There they carved and sewed and sold their beautiful art-work—their ivory work was unparalleled—to any tourists who found their way to town.

When the *North Star* finished its tour of the coast, it picked up the Diomede Islanders to carry them home after their summer in the "city." It was the last we saw of them—or of the great ship—for another long year.

8

Aglagıaqtugut: We Go to School

In the Iñupiat world, knowledge going back ten thousand years was distilled into the culture, through oral tradition, observation, and practice. All of our education was unwritten, continuing a tradition that spanned thousands of miles, from the Russian Far East, through the vast frozen reaches of northernmost North America, and all the way to Greenland.

My family was traditional. We were learning as our forefathers had learned: by surviving in one of the most hostile climates on earth. Most of my relatives, if they could read and write at all, did so at an elementary level. Few had attended school for more than four or five years, which was considered just fine, since the family needed its older children—especially strong young men—to help with hunting, trapping, fishing, and running dog teams.

No one in the family ever mentioned school to me, so it came as a shock one fall day when all my friends disappeared from the beach where we had been playing. Mystified, I walked home and found Nauṅaġiaq, who was busy with household chores. I moped around for a while, then blurted out, "Everyone is gone! Gone to school!" I guess I made a pest of myself, because finally, after trying to change the subject, my mother replied testily, *"Kiikka, kiikka, aglagiagiñ!"* (Go ahead, go ahead, go to school!) So I did. I ran to the Bureau of Indian Affairs schoolhouse in Kotzebue, hung up my parka (not knowing any better, I hung it on the girls' side), and became what we called a beginner.

The BIA school was built for about three thousand dollars around 1900, and forty-six years later, it was definitely feeling its age. For Kotzebue, it was a huge building, second only to the Indian Health Service hospital a few yards away. Still, it contained only two schoolrooms, with the *anaġvik*, outhouse, out back.

In the winter, when the wind blew and the snow fell hard, it was often almost impossible to get to the outhouse. The snow would drift ten or twelve feet deep between it and the schoolhouse, even covering the windows on that side.

You might think that on the roughest days classes would be canceled, but they never were. We were expected to attend school five days a week, and to tell the truth, we welcomed the warmth of the schoolhouse—each room with its own oil heater—after waking up in the chill of our poorly heated homes. It was hard to wake up those mornings, and not just because it was often minus ten or twenty below (when there was even a slight breeze, your skin would begin to freeze almost immediately, so we got in the habit of watching our classmates' faces for white spots, the sign of frostbite). No, what made it so hard was that it was so dark, and we all loved to *pigaaq*—stay up late. Even by the time the school bell pealed across town each morning to let everyone know it was almost 9:00 a.m. and time to be in the classroom, it was still dark. And by the time we returned home in midafternoon, it would already be dusk.

By the 1940s, when I began school, the BIA's educational system—originally designed to assimilate Indians into American life—was functioning very efficiently to eliminate any vestiges of traditional identity and knowledge. Despite the fact that Natives no longer posed any threat to America's existence, there was no stopping the mission to disconnect Native children from their roots. The goal was to isolate children from their cultures, to cut them off from the ancient way of life and leave them stranded somewhere between the old world and the new. From the late 1890s until well into the twentieth century, Native students were forbidden to speak their mother tongues in school (and discouraged from doing so even outside the classrooms). If they slipped, they were punished. Teachers would make them stand in the corner, beat them on the hands with rulers, or force them to write, one hundred times, "I will not speak Eskimo." Meanwhile, their schoolwork deliberately excluded any mention of the ancient music, art, dance, and history of their own people.

Why did our parents permit this? In large part, it was due to an inferiority complex that had grown among our people ever since the beginning of trade with Russia in the late 1700s. Our ancestors recognized clearly superior technology in the goods that arrived from Siberia. Metal knives, pots, matches, nails, axes, saws, and rifles all made life easier than it had been when we had to depend on the more fragile handmade tools of driftwood and timber, bone, ivory, and stone that had sustained us for untold generations. The arrival of these miraculous goods was closely followed by the arrival of Christian missionaries who preached, supposedly for our own good, a degrading message: our languages, cultural traditions, arts, and ages-old wisdom were pagan, sinful, and woefully inadequate. Some of the missionaries brought with them medicines that helped cure certain ailments. However, even that basically benign change had consequences that rippled widely through Native culture, challenging the influence of the *aŋatkut*, our shamans, who traditionally had handled healing.

When Alaska became a U.S. territory in 1867, the federal government joined the churches in their zeal to Americanize the Natives. So much for the "separation of church and state." In 1885, a Presbyterian mission organizer named Sheldon Jackson was named general agent for education in Alaska, and although he was a vocal champion of the Natives, he laid the foundation for the dissipation of their cultures. From that time on, the U.S. government made contracts with various missionary societies, giving them jurisdiction over the education of Alaska Natives, a practice that lasted well into the twentieth century. The missionary teachers set out to make fundamental changes in their "uncivilized" charges, emphasizing, as Jackson wrote, decidedly nonacademic lessons in "honesty, chastity, the sacredness of marriage relations, and everything that elevates man."* The idea was to change and control what Native children learned, and above all to instill orderly western European values prized by the missionaries and the governing authorities (Jackson was paid for his work by both the federal government and his church), while at the same time discouraging the children's attachment to their own traditional cultures.

Report on Education in Alaska, by Sheldon Jackson (Washington, D.C.: Government Printing Office, 1886), p. 20.

Starting in the late 1800s, the federal goverment set up schools in villages like Kotzebue that provided education through the eighth grade. After that, anyone who wanted to continue his or her education had to leave home. Indian boarding schools were established, often in abandoned military bases in places like Sitka, Alaska; Chemawa, Oregon; or Chilocco, Oklahoma. Students from tribes all over the country were sent to these institutions, thousands of miles from their families, for high school education and vocational training. The schools were highly regimented and designed to wean the student from the tribe, teach English, and provide a skill like typing, metalworking, small-engine repair, or carpentry. Many students died of diseases contracted far from home. And many who lived never returned to their families. After graduation, the BIA "relocation" program often sent them to cities like Chicago, Minneapolis, and Seattle, where they often ended up in the poorest neighborhoods because of the menial nature of the jobs.

It was doubtless because our parents loved us so much that they accepted these wrenching changes. They believed their children might have a better life if they just allowed Uncle Sam to provide the tools we needed. So we went to schools where life was completely attuned to the holiday rhythms of the United States of America. We colored turkeys and Pilgrim cutouts to put on the walls, made valentines galore, and drew countless Santas and Rudolphs. In some villages, school officials conducted inspections to see if parents were keeping their homes clean. They sent students over to the hospital and lined us up for shots for this disease or that, took urine samples to check for venereal disease, X-rayed us for tuberculosis, and gave us delousing lotions. I have no idea whether our parents were ever asked permission for all this activity. I doubt it. And even if they had been asked, the notion of civil liberties was unknown to us.

When I started school, of course, I was completely unaware of all this. And for some of us, including me, having a nice, bright warm place to go every day was a godsend, given the cold, cramped, dark homes we were coming from.

My beginner teacher was Miss Eunice Logan, a short, redhaired slave driver with little sense of humor who ran the classroom like a minor general. Even so, I took to the schoolwork from the first. As soon as I learned to read, I read everything I could find or borrow. The school knew better than to allow us to take books or any other paper products home, since anything that could be burned was fair game to be used for kindling. And few of the families I knew possessed any reading material except for comic books, Bibles, and Sears Roebuck catalogs, so that's what I read: comic books, Bibles, and Sears Roebuck catalogs.

Comics were inconceivably precious, and passed from person to person until they literally fell apart. Sometimes we sewed them back together to make them last just a bit longer. We read about the exploits of Batman and Robin, Superman, Spider-Man, Archie, Veronica, and Betty, Prince Valiant, Popeye, and Little Lulu. Those comic books were our television. Bibles, thanks to the Quakers of Whittier, were omnipresent—often large and leather-bound with plenty of space for recording family births, deaths, and other important occasions. And twice each year, every family in town received a huge Sears Roebuck catalog. We would thumb through its hundreds of pages for hours on end, examining and coveting the nice guns, tools, and clothing. And once everyone had had a chance to pore over it, the pages served as toilet paper.

My third year in school, after finishing my beginner and first-grade years, I arrived to find a new teacher in charge. When she asked us to take seats with our classmates, I simply ignored the second graders and went to sit with the third grade instead, since most of my friends were there. A few weeks later, mean Miss Logan came to school to see how things were going. She pointed out to Miss Virginia Powell, our new teacher, that I did not belong in third grade—I hadn't completed the second. But Miss Powell said I was at the head of the class, so they let my self-promotion stand. I must observe, however, that her admiration for my schoolwork didn't keep Miss Powell from whacking me on several occasions with a yardstick to get my attention and set me on the straight and narrow.

For the next few years, I attended school whenever I could—whenever, that is, I was not needed by the family to help with the business of survival. Eventually this sporadic attendance became a problem. School officials began making inquiries about my whereabouts, and it was clear that they looked down on my family for not allowing me to attend regularly.

Once again, my brother Aġnaġaq—Fred—came to my rescue, just as he had in Nome half a dozen years before. After his first wife died along with our father in the food-poisoning incident at Ikkattuq, Aġnaġaq had remarried. His new wife was a woman from Point Hope named Nereid Nash. Nereid was cross-eyed and considered a bit on the grouchy side by the rest of the family. But when she and Aġnaġaq invited me to stay with them in Kotzebue during the school year while the rest of the family went off to camp, I gladly accepted. Somehow she and I managed to get along, and I was able to attend school steadily enough so that the authorities left me alone. I slept on a cot, always lonesome

for my mother Nauṅġaġiaq and the others out in camp. I
never had enough warm clothes and my mukluks had a hole
in the heel. It was not one of my favorite years.

I was a sensitive child, and in those days, as I neared ado-
lescence, all of this weighed heavily on me. I was self-
conscious about the fact that I had a mother somewhere who
didn't want me and a father who had never recognized me. I
understood that I was not a complete member of the family,
and I longed for the companionship of a father who would
love and protect me and teach me about survival and help
me learn about life and girls.

When my brother Tiliiktaq—William—and his wife Mollie had a baby, I was required to take care of her when they
were out partying. There would be no one in the little house
except the baby and me. It grew colder and colder. There
were no lights, no fuel, no food. The poor little baby had no
diapers left and we were hungry. There was nothing I could
do to help either one of us, and we both just cried and cried
until someone older came home.

There were times when I thought seriously about committing suicide. Guns, knives, axes, freezing water, walking out
into the wilderness were all easy avenues to self-obliteration.
However, in the Iñupiaq culture there is one quality that is
considered abhorrent, and that is to *qivit*—to give up. In the
ten thousand years our people had spent in the Arctic, we
had learned the lesson well: this environment was no place
for wimps. And if you quit, you and your family would not
survive. It was as simple as that.

As I look back, I cannot get over the fact that our own people
were so excluded from the workings of the classroom. In my
entire eight years in grade school, I cannot recall a single Iñu-

piaq school activity. When we were in the classroom, it was as if our people did not exist. The notion of having an elder come to speak to us about life and experience didn't cross the minds of our teachers. The human values—the central roles of humility, cooperation, family, hard work, and humor in our lives—didn't even register in the consciousness of the teachers who were trying so desperately to Westernize us. All the wisdom gained during ten thousand years of intimacy with the land and the sea and the rivers and the skies was thrown out the window. All our vast cultural knowledge about geography, animal life, weather, art, the cosmos, music, dance, history, construction, psychology, parenting, hunting—all that was needed to flourish in our world—was left at the door, compliments of a sweetheart deal between the churches and the federal government. We were forced to trade all that for Dick and Jane and Spot and arithmetic.

Children never forgot the message that our language was inferior, that it was inadequate to our future. Year after year, day in, day out, the children of Alaska Natives were told that who they were was not good enough, that they should leave behind the world of their parents and grandparents and become something different.

Yet even today, I have a special bond with the kids I went to school with. We met when we were all innocents—with no idea what life was like in the rest of the world. We dutifully tried to keep up with the multiplication workbooks. We learned to spell. We learned about the first Thanksgiving. We swallowed the cod-liver oil, the malted-milk tablets, and the smooth orange vitamins they gave us with a glass of canned orange or grapefruit juice. They tried to teach us the virtue of time and timeliness.

As for me, I learned. I especially loved to read, and from the moment I had mastered the skill, I read whenever I

could. Despite the dearth of reading material, despite the
meager natural lighting in our sod houses and tents, I read.
In winter, I would take a flashlight into my sleeping bag so as
not to wake anyone, and curl up—preferably with comics or
the catalog, but if I had no other choice, with the Bible. In
summer, I had the twenty-four-hour daylight to help me. I
would lie on the floor with Puya, who helped keep me
warm, and read whenever I had finished my family duties.
And the more I read, the more curious I grew about the
world Outside.

9

Ikayuqtɪ: The Helper

I remember very clearly the day I met Dick Miller. It was a summer morning when I was about eleven, a beautiful day—blue water, breezy, warm—and we were staying in Kotzebue. Everybody in my family was still asleep. They had gone to bed really late because at that time of year it doesn't get dark. I was supposed to help lay some linoleum for some of my relatives, but I couldn't wake anyone up, and so I was hanging around outside their house.

Suddenly a tall, skinny white guy with a thick shock of dark hair wandered over and started a conversation. "Mornin'," he said in a funny accent. "Would you like to work for me?"

Now, the linoleum deal was a volunteer arrangement. This guy was offering to pay me! I accepted without the faintest idea what he was offering—or that this would be a turning point in my life.

Richard Alvey Miller was a young Baptist missionary

who had come to Kotzebue from Mississippi. His church had bought a two-story tarpaper structure in town, a building I knew as the Arctic Adventurers Club, which had been established by one of the most colorful characters in town, a woman named Bess Magids Chamberlain Cross. Her first husband had been my real father's brother, Sam Magids. She was a dynamo. She loved politics; loved to gamble, party, and drink. And she loved to spend money. Eventually she fell in love with the great Norwegian polar explorer Roald Amundsen. In 1928, on the way to marry Amundsen, she got word that he had disappeared while searching for Umberto Nobile, an Italian designer of airships with whom he had flown over the North Pole two years before.

Dick Miller, a not-so-distant cousin of Jimmy Carter, the future president of the United States, had bought the club building with the intention of turning it into a house of God. He wanted me to help clean it out, and apparently he saw something in me that he liked, because over the months that followed, he gave me more paying jobs.

We became fast friends. Dick took a real interest in my fate. One school year I went to Noorvik with Naungaġiaq to help my brother and his wife, who was bedridden with tuberculosis. Dick began to worry about me. I did attend school in Noorvik, but Dick feared that I would fall behind in my studies if I had to go back. So even though he was about to get married, he invited me to stay with him in Kotzebue for the school year since Naungaġiaq would be upriver taking care of Tiliiktaq's wife and baby. I think Dick provided the first regular bed I ever slept in.

When I was twelve or so, Dick invited me to go with him to Fairbanks and Juneau for a convention. Fairbanks was a pretty small town at the time, about 15,000 people—certainly far smaller than Anchorage. But it seemed to me like the center of the universe, huge beyond my wildest imaginings. I found it strange and invigorating.

As we drove from the airport into town, my head was like a swivel, snapping back and forth at the sight and sound of every passing car. I had never been anywhere with automobile traffic—there were no cars at all in Kotzebue then, and probably only fifteen or twenty trucks—and I'd never encountered a modern toilet. I mentioned to Dick that the commode where we were staying was "funny," and he quickly realized what the problem was—and taught me how to flush it.

In Fairbanks, I visited a relative, Sikaaġruk—Al Adams—who was living there with his mother, Sarah. She had been in Nome in the early 1940s with her stepsister, my birth mother, Makpiiq. Like everything and everyone in the city, Al seemed incredibly cosmopolitan. It had never occurred to me that cars had names. Al knew them all, and could distinguish one from another—Ford, Chevrolet, Pontiac! He showed me the even rows of white dots, each about the size of a quarter, on his legs. He'd been run over by a truck when he was younger, which left him with a bit of a limp and those indelible traces of tread marks.

One day, out of the blue, Dick Miller introduced me to my birth mother. He'd heard that she had come to Kotzebue and was trying to find me. Makpiiq and I shook hands politely, but I felt no real connection. Years later, I learned that she had moved from Nome to Fairbanks, and that she eventually had married and borne five more children. Two of her girls were "adopted out"—given to other, more prosperous families to raise, something that was becoming increasingly common. All over Alaska, there are stories of Native babies given up

TOP LEFT: Boris Magids, my birth father, surrounded by his livelihood. I never knew him, and he never acknowledged me as his son. He died when I was three years old.

TOP RIGHT: My birth mother, Makpiiq (Clara), around 1941, when I was born. After leaving Nome for Kotzebue, I saw her only once or twice again.

LEFT: Looking cool on Beach Road in Kotzebue. 1944.

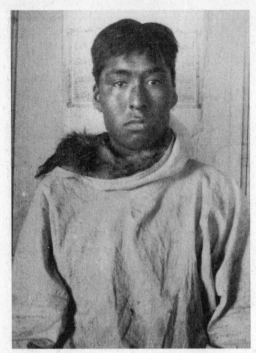

LEFT: Iġġiaġruk (William)—my maternal grandfather and namesake—in his youth, about 1910.

BELOW: Iġġiaġruk with fellow reindeer herders in Kotzebue around 1917. Alaska did not have reindeer until the 1890s, when fifteen were shipped from the Russian Far East. They soon multiplied and became an important source of protein for the Alaska Natives. Iġġiaġruk is seated in the middle, front. Seated in back: Peter Wood, Thomas Weed, David White (whom I knew in the 1950s, when he was very elderly), Eddie Green, Ralph Sampson. In the front, on either side of Iġġiaġruk: Oliver Arnold and Benjamin Arnold.

TOP: A diverse bunch of Nome residents, including Sarah Adams—the stepsister of my birth mother, Makpiiq—on the town during World War II.

BOTTOM: My mother's cousin Aġnaġaq (Fred), who delivered Saigulik (Frances) and me from neglect and squalor in Nome, when we were on the verge of being taken away from my mother by the territorial government that ruled Alaska at the time. He's sitting in front of our house in Kotzebue, with the marshal's house—which doubled as the town jail—in the background.

TOP LEFT: The only photograph I have of my early childhood in Nome. In the back are Makpiiq, an unidentified man, and my aunt Isabel. I'm in the front, along with my sister, Saigulik (Frances).

TOP RIGHT: Aqpayuk (John) and Nauṅaġiaq (Priscilla) at about the time they adopted Saigulik and me in the mid-1940s.

BELOW: Nauṅaġiaq in the early 1940s with four of her eight biological children: sons Auleniq (Isaac), Niŋaugaġraq (Aaron), and Tiliiktaq (William) and daughter Iġvaluk (Ruby).

TOP: A typical Kotzebue beach scene of the 1940s. The three men are weighing seal meat to sell at the trading post. In the foreground are seal pokes—cleaned, blown-up seal skins used for storing a variety of goodies: seal oil, blubber, dried meat, cooked beluga skin, dried fish, and even edible plants. In the background are Archie Ferguson's Farthest North Restaurant, the Arctic Adventurers Club, and the fur warehouses of the Magids Bros (my father, Boris, and his brother, Sam).

(Courtesy of the Autry National Center, Southwest Museum, Los Angeles. Photo no. 26992)

BOTTOM: A spring move on the type of boat that Qaluraq (Lester Gallahorn) used to haul family, gear, and dogs to camp at Ikkattuq. We would often spend six months at camp, so we had to pack very carefully, taking everything we needed to survive—along with a few luxuries, such as comic books.

TOP: Camping on the Noatak River with childhood friends, about 1954. Sitting, from left: Bert Sheldon, Norman Flood, Willard Beaver, Ira Ferguson. Standing, from left: Percy Sheldon, Ernest Norton, Roland Beaver, and me.

ABOVE AND FACING PAGE: Two photos—one of Naunġaġiaq, one of me—taken in front of our tarpaper house in Kotzebue around 1947 or '48. At the right, you can just see the tent we liked to put up in the summer to ease the congestion in the little house. Naunġaġiaq is eating some *maktak* (whale skin) after cutting and hanging beluga meat to dry on the *inisaq* (meat rack) behind her. I am cutting a piece with the *ulu* (woman's knife), and wearing a pair of summer *kamiks*—boots made of sealskin.

(Courtesy of the Autry National Center, Southwest Museum, Los Angeles)

Umiivik, who became a surrogate father to me after Aqpayuk died from eating botulism-infected *utraq* (fermented walrus flipper). 1967.

Naunġaġiaq in her colorful *atikluk*—a lightweight, hooded parka—making bags to hold sand for net weights. Only an inch or two over five feet tall, Naunġaġiaq was strong and tough—she worked tirelessly her whole life—yet was gentle and widely beloved.

for adoption to non-Native teachers, military families, and missionaries. Later, many tried desperately to find their Alaskan families. When they succeeded, they often realized that they were by now so different that they could not fit back into Native society.

That had not been my fate, thanks to Aġnaġaq, who rescued me, and Aqpayuk and Nauṅġaġiaq, who took me in and loved me. And the next chapter in my life was to be out of the ordinary as well.

I finished eighth grade at the Bureau of Indian Affairs school as the valedictorian of my class, and gave a speech entitled something like "You Can Do It If You Want To." The usual course after eighth grade would have been either to attend one of the boarding schools run for Native Americans by the federal government or, more in keeping with my own family's history, to drop out of school altogether.

I'm not sure why I decided not to drop out or go to one of the Native American high schools run by the Bureau of Indian Affairs. Perhaps it was the knowledge that if I stayed where I was, with my family, I would have to work like a dog for the rest of my life just to keep warm and stave off starvation. Perhaps it was all the movies I'd seen at Archie Ferguson's Midnight Sun Theater in Kotzebue. I don't know. What I do know is that Dick Miller helped me find another path: I would go Outside to school. I would enroll at a Baptist boarding school in Tennessee.

I had just turned fifteen and it was 1956. I boarded an Alaska Airlines DC-3 with my carry-on luggage: a paper shopping bag from the N. G. Hanson Trading Company. Nauṅġaġiaq came to see me off, as did my sister Saigulik, older brother Auleniq—Isaac—and little niece Beverly. Saigulik and I were close, and she was sad that I was leaving. She was eighteen, a vulnerable age. She'd had tuberculosis and had never attended high school. By then I was no longer the drag on her social life that I'd been when I was younger, following her about as she tried to enjoy herself with friends.

My mother was sad, too. She was now about sixty, worn down from a hard life. Like Saigulik, who died just eight years later, Nauṅġaġiaq didn't have many more years to live, but I didn't know that. I suspect she had hoped that I would be with her until the end of her life, sheltering her and loving her just as she had done for me. But she never asked me to forgo this wild notion to look Outside, never urged me to do my duty, never pleaded with me not to abandon our traditional life. Looking back, I realize it was an act of characteristic generosity on her part, to allow me to go. Later, when I was almost unbearably homesick for family, friends, and the familiar land that meant so much to me, I would often remember that generosity, and it inspired me to keep going.

I cannot recall whether Nauṅġaġiaq cried when I left. Generally speaking, we are expected to be stoic and soldier through pain, cold, and hunger. As for me, by the time I realized the enormity of the decision I had made, I was way over Kotzebue Sound and there was no turning back.

10

Ausaaqtuŋa: I Go Outside

It is still a mystery to me what led me to head off into the unknown. I could have been a successful hunter. Or I might
have developed some other skills that would have allowed
me to remain at home, marry, and live the life common to my
friends and family. Maybe I could have become an ivory
carver or a commercial fisherman, a bush pilot, a teacher. Instead I departed for an unknown place five thousand miles
from everything I knew. Perhaps it was a bit of rebellion that
drove me on. It is possible that my genetic code contained a
chromosome or two that propelled me to move on to check
out the next headland, the mouth of the unknown river, the
other side of the lagoon—that same impulse that enabled our
people to spread from the Bering Strait across the top of the
earth to Greenland. Perhaps I wanted to show that this little
bundle of rattled nerves and tender sensibilities could face
the unknown and develop new skills and survive.

I knew so little. I knew almost nothing beyond my family,

our life in Kotzebue, and a small radius of the world beyond. I didn't know about the many kinds of peoples who inhabit the earth. I didn't know about the history of America. I didn't know that it had once been wholly occupied by Native Americans and that it then had been overrun by immigrants from abroad. I didn't know about slavery. I didn't know about the Civil War. I didn't even know much about the Athapascan Indians who lived right up the Kobuk River, except that they had once been the enemies of my people.

We knew that some of our villagers had been in Korea, fighting the Koreans. And we knew that the Japanese had been our enemies during World War II. We were told that the Russians were our enemies now, although we didn't have a very clear idea why, or what that meant. I remember the day when I was twelve years old and we heard that some great leader had died. I vaguely thought it was someone in the United States, which seemed very foreign and far away. Much later I learned that the leader who died that year was Joseph Stalin.

In my youth, I was simply too ignorant and unaware to notice the diversity of cultures that surrounded me even in Kotzebue. The teachers who worked for the Bureau of Indian Affairs themselves represented an impressive ethnic spectrum, from Virginia Powell, who was African American, to a Mr. Bielowski—probably Polish—and even a few Athapascans who had managed to get their teaching degrees. (Today, I often think about how they taught and what they must have thought about the BIA educational philosophy, so carefully designed to suppress Native languages and culture.)

Kotzebue's population was similarly diverse. There was Mr. Hugo Eckhardt and his mail-order wife Gretchen, who spoke with a heavy Austrian accent. Louis Rotman had escaped Poland during World War I to avoid conscription in the Polish army. There were the brothers Sam and Boris Magids—my uncle and my father—who were originally from Lithuania. And Swedish Mr. Forslund, who married a lovely Iñupiaq lady who was at least a foot shorter than he was.

To me, however, they were all foreign, all unlike the Iñupiat, so I lumped them together as *naluaġmiut*, our word for white people. Few Iñupiat knew them well enough to have even a hint about their diverse backgrounds. My brother Auleniq—Isaac, the one who carried me from the airport to our house when I first came back to Kotzebue—was one of the very few of our people who was unafraid of dealing with them. A little shy on the *qaqisaq* (brain) side, Auleniq was nonetheless lovable, and he went out of his way to befriend those who visited our village from Outside, often becoming sort of a local guide.

But that was very unusual. Our own identity stemmed in large part from lineage and place and language, and those criteria were not part of the calculus for the *naluaġmiut* who lived among us. They shared a common language— English—and Western notions of politics, economics, and law. We lived in an entirely separate universe of hunting, fishing, trapping, and oral tradition, a culture they didn't understand. There were a few non-Natives who respected the intelligence and Arctic know-how of the Iñupiat, but generally they viewed themselves as superior to us. As I was soon to learn, that was not unusual among the *naluaġmiut* in other parts of the world.

My trip southward from Alaska involved several stops. The final leg ended at Memphis, Tennessee, where Dick Miller's father met me and drove me across the flat farmland down to

Myrtle, Mississippi. Dick's family bought me clothes and introduced me like a little foreigner to their community and their church and to Percy Ray, a famous local preacher who had built a revival center in Myrtle called Camp Zion. To raise money for Camp Zion, Brother Ray preached fire and brimstone throughout the South. And since his travels would take him near my new school late that summer, it was Brother Ray, after traveling about 85 miles an hour, who dropped me off at the Harrison-Chilhowee Baptist Academy in Seymour, Tennessee, where just four hundred dollars a year covered room, board, and tuition. Dick Miller paid some of that amount, and I worked hard at a number of jobs while I was in school to pay for the rest.

On a steamy August afternoon, Brother Ray deposited me and my few possessions in front of the tall white columns of the brick building that constituted Chilhowee's boys' dormitory. Then he drove off in his pink Cadillac to save some souls. There I was, alone in the foothills of the Smoky Mountains.

Harrison-Chilhowee Baptist Academy is in the town of Seymour, Tennessee, thirteen miles from Knoxville, just a couple of miles off the Chapman Highway, which winds up into the mountains. The countryside was like nothing I had ever seen before. In stark contrast to the wild mountains and untamed forests, the icy tundra and stormy coastline of my youth, this landscape featured gently rolling hills, meandering country roads sloping down into valleys spotted with cows grazing by the occasional silo, a small stand of trees surrounding a white clapboard house. Anyone passing through Chilhowee would know it by reading the water tower next to the football field, and a flashing yellow light on the highway warned you were there, but there was no true town center, no village even remotely like my own in Alaska.

Whether it felt right or not, there was no escaping my decision. I had to make the best of it. If I somehow cut the strings to Chilhowee, I would be five thousand miles from home with no possible way to get back to Alaska. So Chilhowee became my home for the next four years.

At first I roomed by myself, which was fine by me. Everything was new and strange—sometimes frightening. One night, a thunderstorm hit. I'd never lived through anything like it. Back home, I remember hearing quiet rumbling in the distance from time to time, but thunderstorms seemed to strike farther inland. Here, the thunderclaps were deafening. The lightning struck so close, I was sure it would hit the building.

I suppose it shouldn't be surprising that the first two classmates to speak to me were girls. They were "community students," which is to say, not boarders. They were local residents who chose (or whose parents chose for them) to attend a religious institution. Jane Self was pale and feminine, with beautiful blue eyes. She lived in a small white house a stone's throw from the boys' dormitory, and she seemed to be a bit more cosmopolitan than most students from the area. Fifty years later I found out that even then she was dying to escape—from Chilhowee, from Seymour, from Tennessee. Ultimately she became a California horseperson. Jane's good friend Jerrilyn Christenberry was, in appearance, Jane's opposite. She had dark hair, freckles, eyes that drooped a bit at the corners, and sensuous lips. My memory of the two of them is as vivid today as when I first met them fifty years ago.

Jane came up to me during orientation and asked me my name. By the next day, though, I'd forgotten her name, and had to ask her to repeat it. "Think of your*self*, and you'll think of me," she said. But the trick didn't work. Her name just didn't come to me, and finally she had to tell it to me again.

I can see now that Jane and Jerrilyn were classic southern belles, a bit on the shy side but wonderfully engaging, and I've never forgotten their kindness in reaching out to a lonely boy five thousand miles from home.

I stood out. Clearly. I was known as the Alaskan, the Eskimo, the Kid from Up North. I had black horn-rimmed glasses and hair with a bit of a bouffant wave. I wore wrinkled jeans with the cuffs rolled up about four inches, held up by my beaded Kotzebue leather belt. I was a sight. I know it. I have pictures to prove it. I looked as if I might have come from some unimaginably faraway place like China, and I think that's what some of my new acquaintances thought. My friend David Burnett, whose family lived in Seymour, said I looked so unusual it was as if I had just stepped off an alien ship.

So far from family and friends and homeland, I wondered whether I would ever fit into this strange environment. But as so often is the case, little by little I got to know my classmates and they got to know me. Danny Allen, my first roommate, was handsome, quiet, gentle, down-to-earth, the only child of a wonderful couple from Bell Buckle, Tennessee. Danny's mother was working toward her teaching degree at Vanderbilt University, and his father drove trucks cross-country. On holidays, at his family's home, we would flush out rabbits for dinner from the piles of brush on his family's farm. He was a singer; his favorite song was "Danny Boy." Forty-five years after I left Tennessee, I got a call one morning from Violet, Danny's mother. She was heading to Alaska on a cruise ship, she said. After hearing me talk about my home those many years ago, she was finally checking it out for herself.

There was so much to adjust to. The food. At home, we had been taught from the time we were tiny children not to be picky, especially when eating out with other families; they might be serving the only food they had on hand, and it would be a terrible affront not to enjoy their hospitality. So I adapted fairly well to the foods of Tennessee. But even I had my limits. Pasta with Parmesan. Forgive me, but it smelled like *miġiaq*—vomit. And pimiento cheese sandwiches! They were a great favorite in parts of the American South, and I will never, ever know why. But pizza and MoonPies—I made my peace with them.

Sports at Chilhowee were also a revelation. Now I was in a world of golf and tennis. I didn't get them. At home, we had no team sports at all. I decided to try out for basketball, and I made the team. I was no whiz, but I enjoyed the brisk workouts, the camaraderie, and the trips to play against rival schools in towns scattered across East Tennessee. Dandridge, Sevierville, Friendsville—the town names still make me wistful.

Imagine this: when I arrived at Chilhowee I had no concept of American football. But I quickly came to enjoy the surging excitement each week during football season and the rallies before the games, and bit by bit, learned to appreciate the finer points of this game, so profoundly different from the skill-sharpening contests of my youth. I spent the first year in the bleachers cheering for the Chilhowee Lions. I couldn't help noticing that the football players—most of them big and burly—looked great in their tight pants, huge shoulder pads, and black jerseys with gold numbers. It also did not escape my attention that they seemed to have the prettiest girlfriends, something I found very interesting indeed.

After a year of watching, I decided to try out for the team. Greg Snyder, one of my best friends at the school, described my debut this way: "Willie had never seen football pads before—had never even seen a football. I thought, *He won't be able to play.* Boy, was I wrong!" I may have been all of 150 pounds, but after a lifetime of work out in the country, I was strong—and very fast. I could run, catch, kick, and tackle; all I had to do was learn the plays, which wasn't easy. But I figured it out, and by my senior year, I was cocaptain of the team, along with David Burnett.

I was very interested in girls, and it was not long before some of them were interested in me as well. Being an "Eskimo" from Alaska made me stand out, and it didn't hurt that I was a good athlete and held my own in class. Over time, I also began to fit in with current fashions. My weird, unruly hairdo graduated to the "flattop" that was wildly popular among my peers. (We used a lot of "butch wax" to keep our hair perfectly still and even.) I traded in my baggy, cuffed jeans for the "pegged" variety, extremely narrow at the bottom, and I wore short-sleeved shirts, rolled up to show off my knotty biceps. All that preening must have done some good, because before too long I began to go steady with a variety of fetching classmates.

Of course, attending a Baptist boarding school didn't exactly offer a wide range of possibilities for libidinous exploration. This was the dawn of the rock-and-roll era, and all of us could whistle the hits of the time, but dancing—along with smoking, drinking, petting, and too much makeup—was considered sinful at Chilhowee. Our "dating" was confined to sitting together at communal meals and spending hours on the phone in endless conversation.

All the same, there was no way the adults could keep a bunch of teenagers entirely apart. We held hands on the way to church and stole kisses while we waited for the weekend mail in the darkened hallways. A side benefit of being an athlete was the bus rides to and from games in other towns. That was one of the few times you could snuggle up a little if you had a girlfriend because the coach and principal couldn't possibly watch everybody all the time. If we were feeling really devious, we might meet surreptitiously in Knoxville while visiting a friend or attending the annual agricultural fair.

In the fall of my junior year, Linda Coolidge arrived on campus. She was unbelievably beautiful, with jet-black hair, perfect teeth, a terrific body—and, in the opinion of Chilhowee's authorities, a tendency to use too much makeup. She had transferred from a far more restrictive school, and perhaps she was cutting loose a bit. Inevitably, I fell for her, and for several months we were inseparable. We broke up during a performance of a play in which we both had parts. In one of our scenes together, I had to hold a baby in my arms, and I was so heartbroken about the end of our relationship that I was on the verge of tears the whole time, and could hardly speak my lines. I didn't learn until many years later that Linda was an American Indian, and that her sister was the singer Rita Coolidge, the wife of the actor and songwriter Kris Kristofferson.

My senior-class girlfriend was Linda Holdman, a blonde from Memphis whose company I enjoyed very much. Over one of our school breaks, Linda invited me to visit her home, a rambling brick house on a slight hill not far from Memphis. Linda's father was a businessman who through grit and willpower had emerged from poverty as a plumber and pipe fitter and eventually built his own business and ran several successful laundries. He was tough and strong, and it was clear to me that he was strict with his three daughters. One night during our visit, I awoke in the middle of the night and sensed Linda's presence in my room. I was scared out of my wits. I was sure her father would blast me away with a shotgun if he found his daughter in my bedroom, and I had no intention of letting her get on the cot with me—the cot that squeaked loudly every time I moved. So I shooed her out of the room. The next day, Linda invited me to ride the family's Tennessee Walking Horse. It was the first time I had ever been on a horse. But I have pictures from that day that look surprisingly good—me riding shirtless, appearing to be pretty much in control.

Lois Reagan, our class brain, became an essential sidekick. She and I worked hand in glove on the class yearbook and the school newspaper. I was taking on more than I could handle, but Lois was always organized and effective—and eventually became a journalist.

I see now that I was being introduced to what was left of the Old Confederacy. The civil rights movement was about to change not only the American South but the whole nation. Through the auspices of Brother Ray, I had been accepted into a world that was about to disappear forever. I attended church, went to summer camp with the Baptists and Methodists, even experienced a full-blown religious revival at Camp Zion. I was there in the bucolic South at a time when girls in lovely, colorful bouffant dresses still danced around the Maypole and there seemed little questioning of the status quo.

I had been at Chilhowee for a year or two when the only other Native American on the school's football team, John Ross Smith, took me home to the Cherokee reservation in North Carolina where his family lived. Until then I hadn't known about the Cherokees. Hadn't known about the Trail of Tears, that forced, horrific march of 1838, when federal troops expelled 17,000 Cherokees from their ancestral lands east of the Mississippi and relocated them to Oklahoma, sacrificing 4,000 Native American lives along the way. On the other hand, I had seen African Americans laboring in the cotton fields under the sweltering southern skies. And when I summered in Mississippi in 1957, I had experienced segregated restaurants and bus depots. I did not really understand segregation. But I was observant. I knew, for example, that I was neither white nor black, and so whenever I rode on a bus in the South, I sat neither in the front with the white people nor in the back with the black people. I always chose a seat right in the middle.

By the time I graduated from Chilhowee in 1960, I was a very different person than when I'd arrived, my belongings in a paper bag. I was definitely someone the Bureau of Indian Affairs would have been proud of. Separated from my tribe for four years, I now spoke a new language and pursued a new way of life. I was spiffy clean, a churchgoer, a sportsmanlike athlete, an A student. I had served as president of my dormitory and my class, had joined the choir and become a fairly accomplished actor. My classmates voted me Best All-Around.

I had battled the loneliness of five thousand miles between me and everybody who meant anything to me by immersing myself in my studies, sports, and friends. I had adjusted to life in a southern state with almost nothing in common with Alaska other than the gritty and enterprising effort it took to make a living. I learned to enjoy fried chicken, grits, black-eyed peas, fried okra, and the occasional possum hunt. They were wonderful years, and thinking back on them floods me with memories. I vividly remember chasing butterflies through a grassy field for Mr. Smelcer's science class. I recall diving deep into the swimming pool to pull the plug among the dead leaves of winter as Danny Allen and I prepared to clean the pool for summer use. I can still feel the excitement that built before a football game and the thrill of using my speed and agility against the opposing team. I was learning to show what I had in me, to be independent, to make my own decisions about my life, my time, and my duties.

But during those formative years, I had missed irreplaceable experiences. I had missed years with my family, hunting, fishing, and trapping—skipped a great deal of learning that could have been of value when I became a man. My southern exposure gave me new perspective on all those things. It helped me to recognize that although the way of life I had known in Alaska was extremely hard, it had produced people with wonderful values and a humanity that made me very proud.

From the moment I flew over the beach at the end of the runway in Kotzebue in August 1956, there was never a day when I didn't think of home. When I was lonely, I thought of the faces of family and childhood friends. I visualized shadows from the full moon on the white snow, remembered the unforgiving winds at twenty below zero, recalled the sight and sounds of dogs straining with a full sledload. I imagined the mirror-calm surface of Kobuk Lake in the never-ending light of summer days, and the aroma of hot sourdough bread emerging from the tank stove. These memories kept me going. And to myself, both silently and out loud, I occasionally spoke our old language, trying not to lose it, attempting to keep it fresh and alive in my mind. *Aarigaa iñuuruni! Nakuuruq mani nuna!* (It's good to be alive! This is a good land!)

No matter where my adventures took me in the Lower Forty-eight, Alaska was always calling. So after graduating from Chilhowee, I headed north, like a salmon heading for the waters where he was spawned.

11

Aksraktautıt: Shıftıng Gears

As desperately as I wanted to return to Kotzebue and see Naungagiaq and my family again, it wasn't easy to tear myself away from Tennessee. I had become part of my friends' lives, and they part of mine. But I needed to go, and I packed my new, old suitcase and headed toward home.

I couldn't afford, though, to get all the way there. I had to stop in Fairbanks, where I would be enrolling at the university, and where I knew I could find work before school began. I needed money.

I took three jobs that summer. The last and best, with an electrical contractor installing a communications site thirty miles south of Fairbanks, offered three dollars an hour. But there was a catch: I had to be able to drive. Could I? asked the guy who recruited me, a friend from church named Bud Smyth, who was a budding dog-musher.

Frankly, the answer was no. There weren't even any roads

in Kotzebue when I was a boy. In Mississippi, that summer I spent with Dick Miller's parents, Dick's sister-in-law had taken me out several times and put me in the driver's seat, but it didn't work. I ended up scaring the wits out of both of us. After enough jerking and mounting the pavement, Dick's sister-in-law finally couldn't stand it. She took a smoke to calm her nerves and drove me home. I didn't tell Bud about that. I fudged the answer to his question. "A little," I said.

With that, Bud led me into a giant school bus that had been converted into a carryall. He showed me the gearshift. "You push the clutch with your left foot, push up for first gear, step on the clutch again to move to second, and so on," he explained.

I looked back into the cavernous vehicle, which was loaded from front to rear with eight-foot half culverts dipped in tar. I was to drive the load past the Air Force base and up a mountain road to the top, where two carpenters would help me unload. Then I would return to Fairbanks.

Bud didn't ask if I had a license. Maybe he knew better.

I was never so scared in my life. It was clear to me that if I didn't get arrested, I was going to wreck the vehicle or get myself killed. But this was my last chance to earn real money before the fall semester. I began to sweat even before I started the bus. I managed to ease it into first and pull out of sight of the company yard; then I inched onto the highway heading south. I drove in second most of the way, following a crude map Bud had drawn. I laboriously made my way to the top of the mountain—only to find it was the wrong mountain. I eased my way back to the highway and finally found my turnoff, but as I neared the top of the mountain—the right one—the bus's engine sputtered to a stop, leaving me at a 40-degree angle, my feet stomped down on the brake and clutch, my hands gripping the wheel for dear life. I don't know how long I sat there, frozen, certain that if I moved, the bus would career back down the mountain.

To this day, I have no idea how I managed to start that engine up again, but I did it. At the top, I found no carpenters. After some time, I began to feel guilty that I was making three dollars an hour for doing nothing, so I unloaded by myself, pulling the heavy culverts out of the bus and lining them up beside the platform where eventually they would enclose communications cables. This, it turned out, was part of the radar system designed to monitor the Soviet Union and provide early warning to America in the event of an attack. I didn't realize until much later that I was a part of America's last defense line against the Russkies.

At day's end, I headed down toward the highway, where I met the carpenters just turning toward the job site. I told them I had unloaded the culverts, and drove off into the late sun, slowly enough that every car on the highway passed me, but feeling wonderful that I was still alive and had earned at least twenty-four dollars. When Bud asked how the day had gone, I told him it had been uneventful and that I hoped I could do it again. Which I did, often.

Looking back, I am surprised that I made it to college at all, let alone found my way through to graduation. I had no idea what I wanted to do with my life, and no one from my family had any academic experience; no one could guide me in this uncharted territory. I had very little contact with my family. My mother Nauṅġaġiaq, who could barely speak English, wrote only a little. When I was a freshman, I got one letter from her, which I have kept through the years. It reads:

Dear Sonny,
I thank you very much for the $10.00 you sent me. I was so
glad to hear from you. Well I am getting old and hardly doing
anything now. I have heard you are coming up to Kotzebue.
I sure am expecting you. I sometimes can't sleep, I would
think about you. When I heard from you I was all right.

I was always furiously treading water, just trying to keep
up enough so that I would be able to regurgitate what I had
been taught in time for exams. And I was always broke, always unsure whether I would be able to find enough money
to pay tuition, room, and board. Not surprisingly, my first
year of college bordered on the disastrous. I made it through,
but even before it ended, I was once again searching desperately for work.

One spring afternoon I noticed a poster on a campus
bulletin board. NORTHWEST ALASKA, it read—immediately
catching my eye with that mention of home—SEEKING ENGI-
NEERING OR MINING STUDENTS, SUMMER JOBS. A number
was listed, and despite having no background in either engineering or mining, I called. The number belonged to an outfit
called the Cold Regions Research and Engineering Labora-
tory (CRREL), and when I told them I was from Kotzebue,
they offered me a job at Cape Thompson, right up the coast
from my hometown. It paid $2.12 an hour, with time and a
half for overtime work between 6:00 p.m. and 6:00 a.m. I
jumped at the chance.

Although I vaguely understood that CRREL was somehow associated with the federal government, I had no idea
that I had been hired to work on a highly controversial operation. "Project Chariot," as it was called, was the brainchild
of Dr. Edward Teller and his Atomic Energy Commission,
and it could have come right out of the script for *Dr.*

Strangelove. We were supposed to drill eight holes into the hard shale just inland from the waters off Cape Thompson, reaming out chambers deep below the surface. Eight atomic bombs were to be stored in those chambers, and ultimately detonated to help excavate the harbor—a demonstration by Teller and company of "peaceful uses of atomic energy."

But I knew nothing of this at the time. I had no idea that the steady stream of academics who visited the site while I was there were largely convinced that the project would have catastrophic effects on the environment—and nearby Iñupiat communities—for decades to come. I was the lowliest of roustabouts on the drilling rig, working night to morning as the rain splattered my glasses and the wind whistled and the drill motors whined, cutting into the shale.

In retrospect, I like to think our little team may have been at least partly responsible for Project Chariot's demise. We managed to complete only four of the eight holes we were supposed to drill that summer, and we found it utterly impossible to ream out those deep bomb chambers: our equipment simply could not cut through the stubborn shale. From my point of view, the outcome was pretty much perfect. That Strangelovian project ultimately collapsed, but in the meantime, I had earned enough money to pay for another semester at college.

But my second year turned out to be even more difficult than the first. And in the always-dark winter months, when for several weeks the temperature never rose higher than sixty below zero, I decided not to return to the University of Alaska for another year. My plan was to spend some time saving money, then to transfer to a college in the Lower Forty-eight.

Returning home to Kotzebue, I rented a small trailer and Nauṅaġiaq moved in with me. It was a wonderful time. The trailer was just right for the two of us, and I was finally able to care for her a bit, to do what I was destined to do when she made me her son. I was keeping her safe and warm, just as she had done for me over all those years.

All that summer, I worked for a tug and barge company, carefully saving my wages. In the fall, I took a job with Wien Alaska Airlines. They started me out writing tickets for children who were making their annual migration to high schools far from home. Later I was elevated to writing tickets for the general public, setting up flights to the outlying villages, and deciding which passengers would fly and how much mail and freight the planes would carry. It was one of the best jobs I ever had, as it involved working with our heroes, the brave bush pilots everyone depended upon to get us from place to place in spite of fog, wind, whiteouts, blizzards, and miserable runways.

By midwinter, I had saved enough money for another semester in college, and I sent off an application to George Washington University in Washington, D.C. Figuring that they couldn't possibly turn me down if I showed up after such a long journey—little did I know!—I set off for Washington in the dead of winter, before I even heard back from the admissions office. On the way, during a stopover in Fairbanks, I stayed with a relative whose husband worked at the post office. Lo and behold, he intercepted a letter to me from GW before it was sent on to Kotzebue. They had accepted me as a student.

I arrived in Washington knowing not a single soul, and checked into a grim, sooty structure at 2100 I Street, an apartment building the university had bought for student housing. After I carried my few belongings (some clothes and books packed in a single suitcase) into the room and looked out the window at the view (another ugly building a few feet away) I almost cried. Here I was without friends, far from everything and everybody I loved, barely able to afford some sheets and a pillow, and looking forward to surviving on two dollars a day. What the hell had I done to myself?

Eventually, however, I began to get involved in my classes. I particularly enjoyed History of Economic Thought and a course in American history, where one of my classmates was Lynda Bird Johnson, the daughter of then Vice President Lyndon Johnson. I also began to meet people. And after a few weeks of living alone, I got a roommate.

Raj Krishan Narang, a student from India, was completely different from anyone I had ever met. Not long after he moved in, I began to notice footprints on the commode and wondered what on earth was going on. It turned out that when Raj went to the bathroom, he stood on the toilet seat, which was the style where he came from. I told him that in America, it was all right to sit down.

When Raj moved on, I got a new roommate—an adventurous character named Gene Roger Harris. Gene had been raised in Enterprise, Oregon, in a family that rode horses and kept cattle and sheep. By the time I met him, he had already traveled to exotic places I could hardly imagine: Morocco, Mexico, India. Gene had a heart of gold. He helped me get through that first incredibly lonely year on George Washington's concrete campus. Little by little, I began to make other friends and to find my way in Washington.

When I wasn't studying, I was at the movies or at the Library of Congress reading Alaskan newspapers to keep up with the news from home. I enjoyed visiting the Arctic exhibit at the Smithsonian, which featured clothing and implements used by our people and explained a way of life deeply

12

Nunavut Tigummiuŋ!: Hold On to the Land!

I graduated from George Washington University in January 1966, and once again, I set out for home. Nothing could have prepared me for what I found there. Where our tarpaper shack once stood, there was nothing but gravel and grasses and weeds; the house had been bulldozed away. My mother, Nauŋaġiaq, had taken refuge in a bare corner of the Assembly of God Church, and the rest of the family was scattered to the four winds. We had lost our little plot of land. This was where the family had come together at the turn of the century; where Aqpayuk's father, Siupsiraq, had raised him, and Aqpayuk and Nauŋaġiaq had then raised their own large family. This was the place where decade after decade the family had tied its dogs, beached its beluga, dried its seal meat and salmon, and moored its *qayaqs* and *umiaqs*. This was where year after year the father and sons would step out on the beach to assess the water, the clouds, and the wind before venturing out on the hunt. We were now homeless in our homeland.

The notion of private ownership was alien to most of our people. We had lived throughout the length and breadth of Alaska, using the land as our forefathers had, becoming intimate with its ways as it nurtured, however grudgingly at times, our existence. We did not think of straight lines and pieces of paper as describing our relationship to the land. We had lived on it, gloried in it. Thousands of years of our heritage lay just under the surface, and the bones of our ancestors were there among them; you could almost feel their presence. We respected that generations of families would return to certain areas as survival necessitated, just as my family did with its plots in town and at Ikkattuq. A house built by the leader of a family would "belong" to him and his relatives in a loose sense, and another family would rarely attempt to occupy nearby land unless they were related. If Alaska's famously inclement weather forced outsiders to use another family's structure, they knew to take good care of it and replace any food or wood they had consumed.

Before Alaska became a state, tribal ordinance had governed places like Kotzebue. The Indian Reorganization Act (IRA), passed by Congress in 1936, set up a mechanism for governing Alaskan villages—the tribal council—that was based on the country's experience with Native Americans in the Lower Forty-eight states. That system, run by Native Alaskans (under IRA rules, non-Natives were not permitted to run for office), didn't change very much the ways we had shared the land for generations.

In 1955, in preparation for statehood, a constitutional convention was held to hammer out a constitution for Alaska. There were fifty-five delegates to the convention. Only one was a Native Alaskan, and he went along with the status quo. The only person who really spoke up for Alaska Natives was actually a *naluaġmiut* (white man). M. R. "Muktuk" Marston was a beloved figure in Alaskan history. He had founded the Alaska Scouts during World War II, companies made up primarily of Native Alaskans that performed heroically and were the backbone of the Alaska Territorial Guard—later the National Guard. He was virtually ignored by his fellow delegates.

With statehood, the governance in Alaska changed dramatically. Tribal councils were no longer the sole governing power in the villages; that was transferred to city councils, which in some places quickly became the domain of non-Natives who finally saw an opportunity to increase their influence in local affairs. It was not long before those councils sought to make sense of the patchwork patterns of property use in Alaska's villages. They asked the federal Bureau of Land Management to survey town sites. First, the BLM determined the total number of lots; then it divided the cost of the survey by that number, thus determining a base price for each lot. After such a survey was completed, federal law permitted individual purchases of lots for homes and businesses.

In Kotzebue, the BLM surveyors had come to town, surveyed the entire three-mile spit from the beach back to the lagoon, then auctioned off hundreds of lots. Later, city fathers told me that they tried to make it easy for people who already occupied a particular plot of land to take formal title by waiving the $25 or $30 average price. Even so, the local Iñupiat never had a chance. Many were out of town gathering food for the winter when the auction was held. Even if they had been present, the concept of "auctions" meant nothing to them, and few had the money to consider participating. In the end, the non-Native community bought up much of the landmass of Kotzebue for $25, $50, or $100 a lot. (Today, those lots sell for $40,000 or $50,000.) The result of the auction was to prevent future generations of Native families from ever owning land, dooming them to be renters or squatters on what was now considered other people's property.

As part of all this, someone had used the law against my family, and we were dispossessed. I was livid when I found out. It was an Iñuk who had bought our land—from my brother. For a bottle of whiskey. The fact that the person was a neighbor and a fellow Iñupiat was particularly hurtful, as this never would have happened had there not been a new land tenure arrangement being foisted on the people. At two o'clock or so one morning, when I was partying with a couple of friends, the man showed up, wanting a swig of whiskey. The minute he and I locked eyes, we were at each other hammer and tong. He outweighed me by a hundred pounds, and I knew that if I let him throw a punch, he would demolish me. So I grabbed him around the neck with my left arm, squeezed as hard as I could, and kept punching him with my right as we rolled around on the floor. Eventually my friends managed to pull us apart, and he left. Later, he claimed that we had ganged up on him. We knew the truth.

Since I had managed to survive in the academic world, had little work experience, limited marketable skills, and, after three years in Washington, was terribly homesick, I applied for graduate school at the University of Alaska Fairbanks. My plan was to earn a master's degree in finance, despite the fact that I never had any finances to manage.

I was accepted, and even though I thought I was headed for financial studies, I signed up for a class on constitutional law taught by the young and brilliant Jay Rabinowitz, chief

justice of the Alaska Supreme Court. I had the impression
that Judge Rabinowitz used the eight students in the class as
a sounding board on issues he was confronting on the bench.

As part of the course, he assigned us a research paper on
any legal subject we wanted to explore, any issue involving
constitutional law. After all the reading I had done as a
homesick undergraduate keeping up with my homeland's
early years as a full-fledged state, I knew exactly what I
wanted to investigate: Alaska's vast lands—and the complex,
vital, and sometimes deeply personal issues surrounding Native ownership.

I took stock of the situation: it was 1966, seven years since
Alaska had become a state, and the fledgling state had a population of fewer than 300,000 and almost no private land to
tax. Delving into the numerous issues regarding the foundation of my state, I learned that virtually all of Alaska was under the control of the federal government. To ensure that the
new state could survive, the act of Congress that created it
granted the state government the right to select up to 104 million acres for state ownership. Not surprisingly, the state officials aimed to pick out the acreage with the greatest potential
for oil, gas, and mineral deposits; they were paying no attention at all to Native interests in the land, and were, in fact,
poised to steal it away from us entirely.

Given that Alaska was officially American now, I wanted
to learn more about the early history of the Lower Forty-
eight, and the first dealings between European settlers and
Native Americans. Those early settlers, I found, used the notion of "discovery" to make claims on the lands they found,
usually paying a small price for the right to control the space,
the resources, and the people of new territories in an attempt
to make the acquisition seem more "legal." I concluded,
however, that the Europeans usually took whatever they

could and slaughtered most indigenous people who had the temerity not to surrender. The result was that after a mere two hundred years of U.S. history, Native Americans outside Alaska had effectively lost an entire continent, and now occupied a total of just 50 million acres in the form of reservations. They had lost all the rest of the land—nearly 2 *billion* acres.

I turned to the history of Alaska in particular, and the key event of 1867's Treaty of Cession, which governed the sale of Alaska by Russia to the United States for $7.2 million. I concluded that, after being handed off from the Russians to the Americans, the Alaskan Natives found themselves in an even more confusing situation. The laws they were required to obey were vague at best, and there were no standards for how they might go about achieving citizenship, or whether this was even an option. More upsetting were the stories I read about non-Natives exploiting these ambiguities to take possession of land the Natives—communal in outlook and new to the foreign notion of private property—had used and inhabited for generations.

There seemed to be some hope, however, in the 1959 act of Congress admitting Alaska to the union. It stated: "As a compact with the United States, said State and its people do agree and declare that they forever disclaim all right and title to any lands or other property (including fishing rights), the right or title to which may be held by any Indians, Eskimos, or Aleuts . . . or is held by the United States in trust for said Natives."

The United States had never won any land from Alaskan Natives in battle. It had never signed any treaties with the Alaskan Natives. Legal precedent was clear: if land had not been taken in battle or seized by an act of Congress, the fed-

eral courts had consistently found that Native Americans re-
tained "aboriginal title" to it. That had to mean that we still
owned most of Alaska!

I knew instinctively that if we permitted the state to begin
to "select" its 104 million acres from the federal government,
we would never be able to retrieve that land. Somehow we
had to stop their selections. Otherwise all we could look forward to would be a lifetime of litigation, ending in settle-
ments of a few cents per acre—similar to those received by
Indians in the Lower Forty-eight—and no land. As I finally
came to comprehend the danger my people faced, it almost
made me ill. If we did nothing, we were going to lose our
land, just as all the Indians to the south had, a century before.

Without control over our lands, our livelihoods, our culture, and our future were doomed, I argued passionately in
my paper, maintaining that aboriginal rights to the land
could be trumped neither by the nascent state nor by private interests. I finished it in the spring of 1966, and Judge
Rabinowitz gave me an A.

A few weeks later, a small news item caught my eye.
Democratic senator Ernest Gruening, one of Alaska's most
powerful political figures, was quoted on a plan to dam the
Yukon River to create cheap electric power. Among other
things, he had said: "What we need to do is pay off the Natives and get on with the development of this land."

I was furious. Gruening seemed so cavalier about Native
rights. But after I cooled down a bit, I realized that the senator's words had broader implications. *Wait a minute*, I
thought, *this powerful leader is actually saying that we have some
rights to this land. If we didn't, why would he want to pay us off?*

I immediately sat down and wrote the senator a letter arguing that Alaska's Natives had the right to decide the na-

ture of any land settlement, and because this was a public is-sue, I sent it to every Alaskan newspaper I could think of. Most printed it.

What happened next nearly scared me—still a starving twenty-five-year-old student—to death. An artist I knew, who had come to Alaska from New York, was also a friend of Senator Gruening. One night, she called me at my dorm and summoned me to a one-on-one meeting with the redoubtable senator. As our mutual acquaintance explained it, he had de-manded to know more about "this Hensley who wrote me a nasty letter about Natives owning Alaska."

I was sweating and nervous as I walked into the old Nordale Hotel in Fairbanks to meet Senator Gruening. I knocked gently on the door of his room.

"Come on in, Willie," he said.

There he was, seventy-nine years old, sitting on the small bed, his intelligent eyes smiling at me and his feet dangling above the floor. He stood up, we shook hands, and he offered me the only chair, sitting back down on the bed.

I respected Senator Gruening's desire to explain to me where he stood, but I knew instinctively that this was a con-frontation. He was a fighter for statehood. In his mind, both the successful evolution of a prosperous state and more than 100 million acres of land that would assure its prospects were at stake. In my mind, this was Native land to which the state had no right unless our rights were first recognized and pro-tected.

"Willie, I saw what you had to say in your letter to the editor," said the senator. "First, I want you to know that I'm the one who ended discrimination in Alaska toward Alaska Natives back in the forties, when I was governor of the terri-tory. I'm the one who encouraged Natives to get involved in politics. Some even ran as Republicans. Not only that, I've pounded on the Secretary of the Interior to do something about this Native land problem and he's done nothing."

He paused, waiting for a response.

I acknowledged his record on civil rights and what he had done to eradicate the NO DOGS OR NATIVES ALLOWED signs that had once been common in restaurants, hotels, and theaters. But then I said my piece: "The Secretary of the Interior can't resolve the land claims of Alaska Natives because only Congress can resolve issues of aboriginal title. The way you and the Congress wrote the Statehood Act allows the Secretary of the Interior to grant away over a hundred million acres of our land. We can't let that happen!"

The senator had another appointment and our meeting ended. I left feeling a little queasy. I knew that the good senator was not going to be an ally of the Natives on this issue. Perhaps he—an assimilationist whose forebears emigrated from Germany—thought we should all just forget about being Native Alaskans and let the country have its way with our traditional lands. More important, though, after all those years of fighting for statehood, he would never sacrifice Alaska to an aboriginal minority. Now that the Natives were beginning to see through the legalese in the Statehood Act, I sensed there was going to be tremendous pressure on the Secretary of the Interior. The powers that be would insist that he allow the state to choose its land, leaving the Natives on their own to figure out how to get compensated—poorly, if history was any guide—sometime in the distant future.

I was in a very difficult place that late spring of 1966. After all my years of study and struggle far from family and home, one single college course had made a huge difference in my life. For the first time, I now understood something solid and serious. I had knowledge and insight that could affect the well-being of 50,000 Native people with whom I

identified. The thought that they, too, might find themselves, in time, in the same situation our family found itself—
dispossessed and homeless—was more than I could bear. I
was bursting to tell them that the land that had nurtured
their existence for ten thousand years was in the process of
being taken away. And these cultures, ancient civilizations of
the New World, were completely unaware of their impend-
ing fate.

But I was powerless and broke. I could pack everything I
owned in the entire world into one suitcase, and couldn't
even afford a bus ride to downtown Fairbanks. Frustrated
and angry, I hitchhiked back to my dorm thinking that we
had no friends in the political world in Alaska. If we were going to succeed in protecting our land, we were going to have
to find a way to fight for it on our own.

13

Tigulugu!: Claim It!

I knew I had to alert the Native Alaskans near Kotzebue—
both my fellow Iñupiaqati and surrounding tribes—about
the danger: if we did not file a claim—and soon—we could
lose our traditional lands to the state, or the federal government, or both. Of course, there was no way of knowing
whether a claim would be recognized by the U.S. Department of the Interior. If the Secretary of the Interior was an
honorable man who took seriously his stewardship of Native
American rights, there was a chance we could protect ourselves. If he was not, we could lose everything.

On May 6, 1966, I wrote a letter to all eleven villages in
the Kotzebue area outlining, as simply as possible, the jeopardy we faced due to the land selection provisions of the
Statehood Act, and suggesting they choose representatives to
meet in Kotzebue to discuss these issues.

I had to borrow ten dollars for the stamps. And I had to
find a way to get home from Fairbanks.

Reva Wulf and Ruby Tansy had been good friends, willing to listen to my ranting about Native land rights as I researched my paper. Reva and Ruby knew that the Fairbanks Native Association—at that time, the only visible Native organization in town—was about to meet. I couldn't attend the meeting, but they agreed to appear on my behalf and ask the group to buy me a ticket to Kotzebue. They came back from the meeting with a discouraging answer: Who, the FNA leaders had demanded to know, *was* this Willie Hensley, and why did he think he should have their money?

Undaunted, I turned elsewhere. I had been introduced by Mike Gravel, then a candidate for the U.S. Congress, to a woman named Helenka Brice whose family ran a successful construction company. Helenka was about five feet tall and abounded with nervous energy, speaking almost incessantly in a gruff, raspy voice. She kindly lent me fifty-four dollars for the trip home.

My mission was clear to me: to try to motivate people to take on the state, the federal government, and anybody else who tried to take our land. The big question was whether anyone would pay attention to me.

The only way to reach people, I figured, was to walk the streets and talk to as many Iñupiat as I could to explain the issue. I also knew that I had to talk to the non-Natives, since they might become alarmed that "Willie was out there agitating." I made it one of my first objectives to minimize their opposition; I was intent on explaining that we were not attempting to take anyone's land away, or to halt development that had a positive impact on the community. But at the same time, non-Natives had to understand that we had a right to some of our traditional lands.

I started with two non-Natives whom I respected, and who I knew understood the rules of the new world that was

beginning to emerge. Edith Bullock, a former territorial legis-
lator, ran the B&R Tug and Barge Company. We had been
friends ever since I worked for her one summer. (In fact, it
was her ex-husband's B-29 bag I'd taken with me when I
went off to George Washington University. For years, it was
my only suitcase.) Edith owned a key piece of property along
the gravelly beach, at a point where the rushing currents
from the rivers that emptied into Kobuk Lake kept the water
deep enough for the tugs and barges. She employed some of
the most competent and respected Iñupiat in the region, and
I knew she could turn a lot of our people against me if she
wanted to. At the same time, her enterprise depended on
good relations with all the people of the region who bought
her products and services. If I could convince her that I was
working for the benefit of the region, she might not work
against me.

Edith heard me out. At this stage, of course, no one—not
even I—knew exactly what we were going to push for.
Would it be land allotments for Natives? Reservations? Native town sites defined by restricted deeds? Would enter-
prises like Edith's be taxed by the tribe? None of this was
clear. I think Edith had a pioneer streak that didn't quite allow her to believe that the Natives would be up to pulling off
a land settlement of the complexity and magnitude required.
But she was also fair-minded, and willing to wait and watch
and see what happened. At least for the moment, she was not
going to fight me or my ideas on land claims. That was a
small victory, but an important one.

The second non-Native I approached was John Cross, a
renowned bush pilot and former Air Force colonel and the
current mayor of Kotzebue. Mr. Cross had been a tenant of
the Friends Church when he first moved to town. (Under the
Missions Act of 1900, a religious denomination could acquire

up to one square mile of land in Alaska, and in Kotzebue, the Quakers had secured the center of the village for themselves.) Then, somehow, he found some land to squat on and he built a home. I remember some controversy about that among the local people. The response from him was that "there had to be a law" somewhere that allowed people like him to acquire property.

John Cross was quiet and unassuming. He had married an Iñupiaq woman from the Shishmaref area, Bessie, and their son Harry had come with me to high school in Tennessee at Harrison-Chilhowee Academy. I had hopes that John would understand what I had to say about land claims.

I had a note from John's city clerk acknowledging that they had received my letter on the history of Native land issues and letting me know that there was a lot of interest in my arguments. I assured John, just as I had Edith, that my aim was to secure land for our people, not to disrupt the economy or scare off development. I told him we would not jeopardize airport improvements or other needed public facilities, but that we were going to push for as much land as we could get and secure compensation for those lands we could not retain. In the end, the mayor was satisfied. He wished me luck and we parted.

Having made my case to these two respected non-Natives, I walked the streets of Kotzebue preaching the message of land claims to anyone who would listen. I was desperate to file a claim, fearing that the state and federal governments might somehow prevent us from protecting ourselves. I knew we had to act as quickly as humanly possible. But in Alaska, among my people, springs and summers are the absolute worst time of the year to have a meeting on any subject. Everyone is at camp, spread out along the coast, lakes, and rivers, working, fishing for the long winter's food resources, picking greens and berries. On that score, I was swimming upstream.

I desperately needed help—and there were so many other obstacles to overcome. Many of our people were employed by the government, the very government we were about to challenge. Here I was, asking people who had long been accustomed to taking direction from the non-Native world to say no to the government. In fact, I was asking them to say "*hell* no"—emphasis critical—to the taking of our land. This was very hard. Our people were not accustomed to confrontation. Over many millennia, we had developed a cooperative working style that smoothed the rough edges from interpersonal relationships so we could live in as much harmony as possible.

Back in Fairbanks, I began planning a June meeting in Kotzebue. I prevailed on the Bureau of Indian Affairs to provide financial support so that representatives from surrounding villages could attend. Bowman Hinckley, who worked for the Bureau of Land Management in Fairbanks, had been a treasure trove of information for me during my research on land rights; he got permission to attend to explain BLM regulations on land title. The BIA agreed to send a representative from Juneau. And when, on June 10, 1966, we held our first informational meeting at the BIA school in Kotzebue, about seventy-five people showed up. Delegates came from all over the region—from Ambler, Noatak, Kiana, Kivalina, and Kotzebue.

We translated our proceedings into Iñupiaq. First, I laid out the situation that faced us as simply as I could. Then, for about four hours, the delegates discussed the matter. Finally, I asked those assembled what we should do about our traditional land. Almost in unison, they cried out: "Claim it!"

I took a big black pen. On a simple Kroll map of Alaska, I

drew a circle encompassing about 30 million acres—all the areas that drained into the Kotzebue Sound. "Okay, here is our claim on behalf of our thirteen villages," I declared. Then I drafted a letter on behalf of the Northwest Alaska Native Association, which we formed expressly for this purpose, and signed it, along with everyone else who had participated in the meeting.

When it was over, I breathed a sigh of relief. At least for the moment, the state and federal governments were on notice. We had put our stake in the ground. If any entity, private or public, wanted land in our region, they would now have to deal with the claimants on petition number 035294: the Iñupiat people of the Kotzebue region.

14

Arguaŋaruaq: The Militant

The summer that followed the filing of our claim was one of the most frenetic of my life. Establishing our rights to the land became the defining issue not just for the Iñupiat, but for the Yupiat, the Athapascans, the Aleuts, the Tlingits, and the Haida—all the Native peoples across the huge new state. The organizational and political challenge was enormous. We had no money, no organization, no communication system, no roads, no useful contacts, no powerful allies. We had to overcome cultural differences, vast distances, and long-time rivalries in order to unite.

In retrospect, I can see that I was an angry young man. Everywhere I looked, there were problems that needed to be solved. Here, in the coldest part of America, there was hardly any decent housing. Year after year, the wind whistled through our miserable shacks, shacks that had no plumbing, no safe water. Outside the major towns—Nome, Bethel, Kotzebue, and Barrow—there was no health care, no support for the elderly or the infirm. There was no electricity to provide light for the ceaseless work required to keep us alive or refrigeration for our protein-intensive diet.

Our children were being taken away at a tender age and sent hundreds or thousands of miles away to be educated in a curriculum in which no parent had any say. There were no training programs of any consequence to help us make the transition between the old world of subsistence living and the emerging resource economy. In the institutions that affected our lives—the courts, the schools, the hospitals, the bureaucracies regulating fish and game—the voice of the Iñupiat and other Alaskan Natives was barely a whisper.

This was our land, our home. We constituted by far the majority of the population in northern and western Alaska. Yet for all practical purposes, we had no say in what happened to us. It seemed to me to be the challenge of a lifetime. Yes, I was angry. I was angry at the poverty we lived in, the illnesses that ravaged us, the constant hunger among us, and the bloated bureaucrats who flew into town, assuming we were ignorant. I remember the planeload of BLM functionaries—from the state director on down—flying into Kotzebue from Anchorage in their government plane to meet with me after I complained about our people being snookered out of our land. This "shock and awe" approach—sweeping in, in overwhelming numbers—was, to me, a clear example of their bullying tactics.

As a high school student, I had observed the remnants of slavery in the South—the separate drinking fountains and accommodations, the drudgery of the blacks in the fields. And in college, during the summer of 1965, I had traveled to Poland and there witnessed the repression of the Polish people by the Soviets and the Communist party. I remember the wrinkle-faced, ragged peasants in Poland climbing onto the sooty trains with their hard wooden benches, catching the train into Warsaw to sell chickens and vegetables. I saw a joyful block party celebrating the fact that a family had won permission to go to America turn somber, fearful, simply because a member of the party had suddenly appeared down the street. Was there ever any hope for a better life for the people of Poland in the grip of the party and of Russia? All these experiences underscored what I, as an Iñupiaq, was beginning to piece together: the three-hundred-year-old system that had taken control of the Indians in the Lower Forty-eight was now being used to cement control over our people.

Occasionally I got into fistfights in my youthful rages. Sometimes I felt that our people had become so dependent on the *naluaġmiut* that there was no separate will left among them, no one capable of challenging the way things were. Our people had grown so accustomed to the laws and rules that had governed us for more than a century. We were used to obeying the priests and the government agents who made those laws and rules. The very idea of change was uncomfortable for everyone concerned. At this point in our history, our own leaders were not about to take on both the state and federal governments and the powerful business interests that were so avidly eyeing Alaska's riches—riches that very likely lay in our traditional lands.

But I knew that things had to change, and I was determined to make a difference. I had nothing to lose—no job, no house, no wife or children—and I gave it everything I had. The anger fueled my pent-up energies during the summer of '66. Militant though I was, it was clear to me that we had to work within the system. If we were going to make changes, we had to learn to use political tools our people had mostly ignored. So perhaps it was inevitable that when everything began coming to a head, I decided to run for the state House of Representatives. Even if I did not win, I figured I might perform a little service—something like Paul Revere galloping through Massachusetts warning about the coming of the British. I could campaign from village to village and warn all the Native Alaskans that our homeland was at stake—in danger of being taken right out from under us by the state, an entity that had been created by people who understood little of our lives and circumstances.

Both parties tried to win the Native vote in the elections of 1966. And all of a sudden, as it turned out, the Natives were very, very interested in the political process. And because of them, I won. I vividly remember biking up to the Alaska Communications System office late on August 23, 1966, to check on the radio reports that were filtering in on the voting in the far-flung villages. It was quickly apparent that the results were lopsided: I was running away with the vote in the Democratic primary election. I'd run as a Democrat for entirely pragmatic reasons. Under the electoral system, I had to choose a party—and it was almost impossible to win as a Republican from the bush. Ever since the FDR days, Alaska had been largely and staunchly Democratic. I would have preferred to run without a label and to work the way we normally did in our villages—through consensus. And once I got to Juneau, that was the way I approached my job, trying to get my colleagues in both parties to focus on the issues that needed attention. But since the Democrats almost always won the general elections in that part of the world, I joined their party.

I was filled with joy at winning. This meant that all those years of loneliness and isolation in search of an education had paid off, and the Iñupiat people were willing to give me a chance to represent them. They trusted me to do all I could to make improvements in their lives. I took this trust very seriously, and began two decades of working day in, day out on the panoply of issues that confronted us.

The most pressing issue of the moment, of course, was still the land claim. In October, we were able to pull together a good showing of representatives from my own people and various other Native groups throughout Alaska, and we created the Alaska Federation of Natives, the first pan-Alaskan organization to successfully cover the entire state. I chaired the land claims committee at our first convention and wrote our position statement on the issue, essentially arguing that there was no "public land" in Alaska. It was all Native land unless there had been a previous taking by the federal government for federal use. And if there had, then we were owed compensation.

By November, when I was formally elected to the state House of Representatives, I'd become a public figure. Everyone in Alaska who heard the news or read the papers knew that a young, bespectacled Eskimo was going to Juneau in January. I wasn't the first Native Alaskan in the legislature, but there had not been many others, and I was certainly one of the first of my generation. Earlier Native legislators had been Americanized, accepting of the status quo, and unwilling to fight for their people's land. The new generation was different. Backed by passionate supporters, we were determined to use our youthful energy to make major changes.

My new role provided several advantages. For one thing, it gave respectability and status to the fledgling Native organizations—the Northwest Alaska Native Association and the Alaska Federation of Natives—I'd recently helped found. Most involved in the land claims debate were in our twenties. We were proposing some big reforms, without the imprimatur of our elders, and anything that lent us legitimacy was important. And there was another advantage—

less philosophically important but essential all the same: for the first time in my life, I no longer had to live hand to mouth. I was going to have a regular income—five hundred dollars a month!

Until then, my experience working for money had been a little meager, to put it mildly. In Kotzebue, I had emptied what we so charmingly called "honey buckets" and swept floors at Pete Lee's pool hall, dumped garbage for the Farthest North Restaurant, done odd jobs for Dick Miller, spent two days as a movie extra running down a snowbank with my classmates to meet a bush plane, worked as a clerk and stocker for Hanson Trading and in the shop at B&R Tug and Barge. At Chilhowee Academy, I had cleaned a floor of the boys' dormitory, weeded tobacco patches for fifty cents an hour, and had the washing and drying monopoly in the dorm for anyone who would pay me twenty-five cents a load. In the District of Columbia, I'd worked as a typist for the Bureau of Indian Affairs. In Fairbanks, I had served as a day laborer and been on a small drilling rig.

I have often been asked why I decided to run for the legislature when I was so young. What made you think that you had a chance to win when you had been away from home for ten years and barely knew anyone other than your family and friends in Kotzebue? Were you not running against adults with real experience who had lived in the district all their lives? What possessed you to take this path?

The primary motive was my hope and prayer that I could do something about preserving the Native land. But the truth is, there was more. I knew intimately the daily living experience of our people. As a youngster, I had experienced neglect, hunger, and cold. I understood the hard work it took to survive in the wilds. I knew the intimate details of keeping warm and dry and the pain of sickness without medical care. I understood what it was not to have the money to buy the bare essentials of daily life. I knew how much labor it took to trap, skin, and dry the furs that brought in needed cash.

As a student, I had become aware of economic systems, the mechanisms of land tenure and ownership. I had studied political systems and governance and a bit of philosophy. And I had begun to see that our people had virtually nothing to say about the most important things that affected our lives. No one in authority paid attention to our language and how valuable it could be in helping ease our people into the changing world we were a part of.

When a doctor operated on one of us, there was no one on the staff to tell us in our own language just what was being done to our bodies. When the flight attendants made their announcements, they did it in English and many Iñupiat did not comprehend the safety issues being discussed. It was as if our people and language didn't exist.

No one understood how we had governed ourselves for ten thousand years. Rules were being made for us by people whose mandate was to change us by attacking the very essence of what made us unique: our languages, our names, our religion, our customs, and our values.

My goal was to see our own people participate in making decisions that affected their lives and their children's lives. Inexperienced as I was, I sensed that the key was to gather facts, learn the rules, press hard, make alliances, fight for position, and be respectful, but above all to build the Native power base as strong and as united as we possibly could. This game was new to us, and we had to play it very seriously.

15

Sakuuktuŋa: Working Hard in Juneau

Now, all at once, I was twenty-five and representing a district the size of Texas, and I was too inexperienced even to know how unusual all of this was. I suspect that when I was first elected, Republicans and Democrats alike had braced themselves for some raving radical who was going to make all kinds of waves, rant about the terrible things that had been done to the Natives, and generally make pioneer Alaskans feel miserable about their lack of concern. ("Pioneers" were white Alaskans who had come up in the Gold Rush years or shortly thereafter; being one gave you bona fides as a "true" Alaskan, unlike those who came later.) After all, this was the 1960s. The civil rights protests were in full swing, the era of identity politics was coming into its own, the rallies against the Vietnam War were going strong, and the Free Speech Movement was galvanizing students across the country. Would Alaska face similar protests?

If that's what they expected, they didn't know much

about the Iñuit people or Alaska Natives in general. While we were passionate, we were not fools. Deep down, we knew that we could not cut off the hand that fed us or destroy any bridges—real and theoretical—we might need in the future. Besides, we were scattered to hell and gone over four time zones across Alaska (it was not until 1983 that the state finally decided to move most of its territory to a single time zone)—not a good recipe for large organized protests.

Perhaps because we were a new and poor state, we scrapped over what little money there was to spend. We would conduct committee meetings with a single staff person. We drafted our own legislation. Then we danced and partied late into the night and got up early in the morning to posture for the press. It was unlike anything I'd ever experienced before.

Still, it was clear to us all that it was time for the state to take some responsibility for the living conditions of Native peoples. My colleagues and I pushed to change the laws that prevented Alaska Natives from being cared for in the Pioneer Homes for the elderly, and we had one built in Kotzebue. Native Alaskan children who went to high school still had only the option of attending one boarding school in Sitka, or two in the Lower Forty-eight. I sponsored legislation that enabled us to build three high schools in my district, and we pressured the state to bring our children back from the Lower Forty-eight BIA boarding schools. I pushed for changes to permit nonprofit liquor stores, so that revenues from liquor would stay in the villages. And to get us in touch with the rest of the world, I helped establish local nonprofit radio stations. The second one was established in Kotzebue as KOTZ (with the slogan "I've got the hotz for KOTZ"). I introduced the Alaska Rent Review Act to keep a lid on rents during the construction of the Trans-Alaska Pipeline, when 20,000 new

workers from Outside descended on the state. I even sponsored what came to be called "no booze for bigots" legislation to prevent the granting of a liquor license to any
organization—mainly Elks clubs and other private organizations—that discriminated on the basis of race, and made
most of their money from selling alcohol.

Among the *naluaġmiut*, a certain territorial mentality
about "the Natives" prevailed. There continued to be the
sense that we were Uncle Sam's business and not really the
concern of the state government, even though we were also
citizens of Alaska. The new state relied on the federal government to provide hospitals, schools, welfare, training,
housing, sanitation, and transportation of goods to the village people. And the governor expected any federal funds to
flow through his office, so that he could influence how it was
spent and who did the spending—and take credit if something useful happened to be accomplished with it.

The state was not about to provide services that it didn't
have to for tens of thousands of its citizens who were scattered in villages over its 365 million acres. Hell, the state government couldn't even take care of the citizens it had in the
urban areas. With a paltry budget, almost no money coming
in from tiny private property taxes, and a small population
spread over a gigantic area, the state was limping along on
what little money it had, and wanted to leave important issues like schools, health care, and roads for its Alaska Native
population up to the federal Bureau of Indian Affairs. It was
going to be a long, hard slog to make changes in the way
business was done in Alaska for Native Alaskans.

The beauty of the American system is that you get to
speak. And I had a lot to say. Few Alaskans really understood
the nature of life among village people. Hardly any visited
the villages in the summer, let alone the winter. Most knew

nothing of our culture, despite having spent their lives in Alaska. My Native colleagues and I had a dual challenge: to unite our own people and also to educate the urban citizens—to demonstrate to them that we deserved a fair share of the land we had occupied since time immemorial, and an equal part in the services other Alaskans enjoyed.

So I learned the rules of procedure and the courtesies that are a part of the political process. I worked both parties tirelessly. I made speeches on the floor of the state House and Senate, in committee rooms, and at conventions.

There were times when I was angry to the point of tears about the conditions we were trying to change and the urban legislators who would not budge. We were a minority throwing roadblocks in the way of a majority that had high expectations of wealth and self-determination once statehood was achieved, and many of them resented what we were trying to do. But remarkably, the system did respond. Perhaps not as quickly or as generously as we would have liked, but it did respond.

Juneau was then a small city of just over 20,000 people at the base of 2,000-foot mountains along the shores of Gastineau Channel. The city once had America's largest gold mine, but the gold had long played out and now its major business was government. There wasn't enough space for the legislators streaming in from all over Alaska when the legislature met from January until April, May, or June, and we frantically scrambled for housing for the three-to-six-month sessions. It was the sort of place where it was impossible not to run into someone you knew, because the entire town clings to the base of the mountain, and all the restaurants and bars are on Franklin Street, the main drag.

I was running in forty different directions between my legislative duties, the Northwest Alaska Native Association

(NANA), the Alaska Federation of Natives, and the land claims movement. I even served on a committee known, I am almost certain, by the longest acronym in history: Project NECESSITIES (National Education Committee for the Effective Social Science Instruction and Teaching of Indian and Eskimo Students). And along the way, I was elected president of the Alaska Village Electric Cooperative—in itself a monumental task.

I had not a single staff person to help with this blizzard of duties. I was like a whirling dervish, trying to serve my constituents, keeping the fledgling NANA going, building up the AFN, trying to electrify the villages, and bringing our children home from the boarding schools. And always, underneath the clamor of other issues, was the one that mattered most to me: the battle to preserve our land.

As a social animal, I was a bust. Friends would invite me home to dinner and I would literally fall asleep on the floor. And I was not alone. Our regional leadership was stretched in all directions. Most had to work for a living and provide for their families while at the same time attempting to preserve the land of our forefathers from the state, federal, and petroleum industry juggernaut that was being unleashed. We had the proverbial polar bear by the tail, and it was hard to hold on. Most of us were ill prepared for the responsibilities we had certainly asked for. We were young, we barely understood the American political system, and our opponents outclassed us on almost every score. But we had two crucially important assets on our side: an excess of passion and, to sustain us throughout, a fundamentally optimistic outlook.

16

Aŋuyaktugut: Battling with the Great White Father

Those of us, mostly young people, who were struggling to build the Alaska Federation of Natives wanted it to be a credible organization that represented all the tribes and villages of Alaska. Some of us were urban now, and had been schooled in Outside universities and technical schools. But our identity had been forged in our villages near the Arctic coasts, along the banks of the Yukon, among the timbered fjords of southeast Alaska, or in the fog-shrouded, rocky, treeless Aleutian Islands.

By 1969, three years into this enterprise, we were barely able to maintain a real AFN office, or to pay our president, an Athapascan Indian named Emil Notti. Emil had been raised in the Koyukok River area, the son of an Italian father and an Athapascan mother. He had earned an engineering degree, and in the 1960s became head of the Cook Inlet Native Association in Anchorage, the host for our first meeting of the

AFN. Short, handsome, and respectful, he was the perfect face for a statewide native organization.

Despite our lack of experience and resources, in staking a claim to the traditional Native lands and trying to stop the state from taking our land, we were determined to take on the state of Alaska itself, the federal government—and, in a way, our own village and tribal leaders. It was not that we did not respect our leaders. It was more that we saw something they could not see. Or perhaps they saw it, but they didn't believe that our people could win this battle.

The Natives of Alaska had laid claim to virtually all of the territory defined in the Statehood Act, basing our claims on aboriginal title and seeking a settlement from the Congress of the United States. The filing of our land claims had brought disposition of all lands to a dead halt, preventing the state and third parties from taking ownership of any land. Stewart Udall, the Secretary of the Interior, had come down on our side, ruling that no land claimed by Alaska Natives could be disposed of—by the state or by any third party—without the consent of those who had claimed it. Without that action, we would have been dead in the water. Udall, with roots deep in the American West, in my mind had the face of a chief. He was anathema to developers, but for us, he was a savior. Without his decision on the land freeze, our effort would have been hopeless.

This was no small matter. At the time, the infant state was an economic basket case, running a deficit government with little revenue from the tiny population, just about 226,000 people at the time, and very little private land to tax. State officials could see the answer to their problems right in front of them—the gold at the end of the rainbow, the holy grail, and the Big Rock Candy Mountain all rolled into one: the 10 billion barrels of oil that had been discovered in 1968

in Prudhoe Bay, smack-dab in the middle of my Iñupiat con-
stituency's homeland. All that stood between them and development of that potentially revenue-rich resource were
these troublesome Native land claims. Not surprisingly,
Alaska's government and everyone else who had a stake in
the new state's success were doing everything in their power
to get us out of the way.

We had no intention of budging. Between 1966 and 1971,
our Native leadership focused nearly single-mindedly on
the land claims. Early in 1967, for example, we learned that
Alaska's congressional delegation and Governor Walter
Hickel were going to meet with Secretary Udall in Washington to decide what to do about the Native land claims. We
knew darn well that the state was going to try very hard to
ram through its land selections, trying to secure most of the
potentially lucrative land for state use.

We had not been invited to the Washington meeting, but
Emil Notti and I nonetheless decided that we should attend.
We scraped together small contributions—five dollars here,
ten dollars there—from anyone we could persuade to support us, and flew all night, headed to the District of Columbia, where we more or less stormed the session. We informed
the Great White Fathers assembled there that this land was
Native land, and that the Statehood Act granting 104 million
acres of land to the state was in violation of the Organic Act
of 1884 (passed in response to gold miners who wanted to
have a legal right to their mining claims). That act had also
promised protection of Native land rights. It was the duty of
the Interior Secretary to protect us, we argued, and Congress
was obligated to resolve the issue.

That was the first of more than 120 trips to Washington I
made over the next five years, each trip taking almost
twenty-four hours each way. We would fly all night long,

catching what sleep we could on the plane, then check into fleabag hotels within walking distance of the Capitol, cramming as many of us as we could into a single room. There we'd shower and shave, dress in whatever wrinkled slacks and shirts we had, and head for Capitol Hill for a day of lobbying. Toward evening, we would meet for a beer, have dinner, and party into the morning—then catch a few hours of shut-eye before heading back to the Hill.

It was an exhausting life, and it took its toll. Incomes plummeted. Some of our leaders lost their jobs or were roundly reprimanded for espousing a cause their employers believed was strangling the infant state. Wives became alienated from husbands and children were neglected in their tender years. Divorces ensued.

My own first marriage was one of the casualties. I had met April Quisenberry in Juneau, where her family had moved from California; she worked for one of my colleagues in the state legislature. We married in 1969 and moved to Kotzebue, where we rented a typical village home—no water or sewer—and I promptly left on a three-week business trip. April came to Juneau when the legislature was in session, and her father and I bought a modest house there that included a small apartment for us. But even in my newly married state—and even after I was elected to the state Senate in 1970—my travels continued unabated. It was a hard life for April, and I don't think she was ever happy about having to live in the village. Her interests expanded beyond the confines and constrictions of village life, and by 1971 we were estranged. In 1973, we divorced.

Despite the personal hardships, we kept at our work on the land claims—almost nonstop. Always, our message was the same: Alaska Natives had a right to the land and must have a say in how any settlement was designed—whether we should get land, cash, or a combination of the two for whatever we might cede to the state of Alaska. Ever since writing my paper on land rights, I had realized that it would be easier for the federal government to offer cash for our land than to offer the land itself. That, after all, was the American way, going back through centuries of interaction with Native Americans. From the start, the nation had wanted the land and its riches and had taken it. We knew it would not be easy to get Congress to convey it to us.

When I look back on those years, I realize how very little we knew about the ways of the world, even though we were confronting it head-on. None of us had the faintest idea how power politics really worked. We had no experience at all with public relations or the press. But we learned on the fly, and I look back on many of the lessons with considerable amusement.

One of the first things we had done in 1966 after forming the Northwest Alaska Native Association—part of our effort to establish NANA as a presence to be reckoned with—was to endorse candidates for office. We endorsed Bill Egan, the Democratic incumbent, for governor. He lost by a hair to Republican Walter Hickel. And we endorsed Democrat Mike Gravel, who was running against an incumbent, Ralph Rivers, for the U.S. House of Representatives. He lost. However, we endorsed Gravel again in 1968, when he ran for the U.S. Senate against the formidable Ernest Gruening, my former nemesis on the land claims issue. This time Gravel won.

As a senator, Mike Gravel wasted no time making a name for himself. He endeared himself to the Hollywood crowd, and eventually to the antiwar movement, despite having been elected as a hawk. He endeared himself to us as well.

He listened to our ideas and took our suggestions seriously—more than we got from most candidates.

Alaska's other senator, Ted Stevens, was appointed to the job in 1968 by Governor Hickel after his predecessor, Senator Bob Bartlett, died of heart failure. Stevens, a Republican, had been a colleague of mine back in the state House of Representatives, and he was one of the few lawyers in Alaska who understood the seriousness of Native land issues, having worked in the Interior Department during the period when Alaska became a state. He and Mike Gravel hated each other, and at first we worried that Senator Stevens might be too close to Governor Hickel, who had fought hard against Native land claims when he became governor. In the end, however, both Stevens and Governor Hickel himself became positive forces for our land settlement.

Senator Gravel, as it turned out, gave us our first real taste of big-time national politics. In the mid-1960s I had become very good friends with Sam Kito, who had been born down in the panhandle of Alaska in the southeastern part of the state, a long way from Kotzebue. Sam's mother was Tlingit and his father a Japanese émigré who worked in the canneries. Sam strongly identified with the Alaska Native community, a tricky business down in southeast Alaska—especially in a place nicknamed "Little Norway" because of the large number of fishermen from Scandinavia. Although he had been educated in electronics, courtesy of the Bureau of Indian Affairs, he had given up a well-paid job tracking satellites to work for the Fairbanks Native Association at half the salary. He also ran for the local school board and won. He was being ensnared by a duty that is impossible to resist in the Alaska Native community—service to his people.

One weekend when Sam and I were in Washington lobbying for our cause, Gravel's staff invited us to come along on an outing: a canoe trip on the Shenandoah River. Neither of us had the proper gear for such an outing but we were young and open to anything. More important, we were learning that in order to have our voices heard, we had to have good access to those in power, and the key to that was good relations with Hill staffers. So off we went on a glorious sunny Saturday.

The staff put Sam and me in the same canoe. We didn't let on, but neither one of us had ever been in a canoe. Canoes were Athapascan. My people had *qayaqs* and *umiaqs,* and in Sam's part of the world, they used huge seagoing vessels made of cedar. But we were good sports and we piled in, Sam taking the bow. It was, of course, a fiasco. Before long, the two Alaska Natives—great outdoorsmen, everyone thought—flipped our canoe in what was barely white water. It was so embarrassing. Later, when we got back to our hotel, Sam made an observation that has stuck with both of us for forty years: "Willie, I don't think paddling a canoe is genetically passed on!"

The next day, we had been invited to Senator Gravel's home in Maryland. But that very morning, there was a scandalous article in one of the local papers that was soon all over the news. It alleged that the senator had exchanged his vote for sex on a yacht belonging to a member of Congress. Sam and I almost decided not to go to the Gravels', since we figured he would be completely out of sorts because of the awful press. But our curiosity finally got the best of us.

This was the first such social affair Sam and I had ever been invited to, and we didn't know quite what to expect. We were just learning the ropes, and mostly hoped that we wouldn't use the wrong fork or say something stupid.

Gravel himself opened the front door and greeted us as if he didn't have a care in the world. He invited us in and we said hello to Rita Gravel, a darling of a woman perfectly suited to her new role as a senator's wife. The party was in full swing and it was as if we were in a cocoon, comfortably insulated from the embarrassing news swirling around outside. It was our first exposure to something Washingtonians live with as a matter of course and learn to take completely in stride—controversy, scandal, and negative press. Over on the tennis court was Jack Valenti, the longtime head of the Motion Picture Association of America and one of the most influential voices in the nation's capital. Powerful senators and congressmen were scattered all about, chatting and enjoying themselves. Sam and I tried to seem as nonchalant as everyone else as we joined the party, sipping wine and checking out the hors d'oeuvres. We knew if we wanted to keep our land claims and other issues front and center, we had to rub elbows with the high and mighty. We had to let them know that we weren't radicals and our issues were reasonable and just.

A footnote about my friend Sam Kito: Years later, when we began to focus on what I call the "inner world"—on maintaining Alaska Native spirit and identity—I used to encourage Sam to focus on his cultural heritage. One day he called me up with good news.

"Willie, I'm taking your advice," he said. "I've signed up for language classes."

I was overjoyed. The Tlingit language was in serious danger of dying out in southeast Alaska. I applauded his decision and congratulated him. Then I asked when he would start his Tlingit classes.

His response almost knocked me over: "I signed up for Japanese!" he said.

"Sam, that's wonderful," I told him, recovering as quickly as I could. "We need Tlingits who can communicate with our allies."

There were a few times when the powerful came to us, rather than the other way around. One such occasion was in late 1969, when a bipartisan group of senators, including Mike Gravel, Ted Stevens, Walter Mondale, and Ted Kennedy, came to Alaska. The occasion was a trip sponsored by the Senate's Special Committee on Indian Education. Senator Kennedy had assumed leadership of the committee after his brother Robert was assassinated in 1968; this trip, in fact, had been planned by Bobby Kennedy himself.

Both Emil Notti and I were invited along as the group toured villages throughout the state and met with the local people. And when a faulty generator marooned us for a while in Arctic Village—an outpost in Athapascan territory up in the Brooks Range—I had a chance to talk with Senator Kennedy one-on-one.

After we had finished meeting with the villagers, he and I took a walk, ending up at the small spruce-log Episcopal church. I seized the opportunity and began to tell Senator Kennedy about our land claims struggle. I told him how desperate we were to protect our homeland from the inroads possible under the Statehood Act. I told him how much pressure we were under from the state of Alaska, the oil industry, the miners, businessmen, and everybody else who thought their interests were going to be adversely affected by our claims. It was a heaven-sent opportunity to get our message across to someone who might later make a big difference.

That same year, Mike Wallace of CBS television's newsmagazine *60 Minutes* decided to focus his attention on

Alaska. He had set out to do a story on the big oil rush that was taking place at Prudhoe Bay. But due to bad weather near the North Slope, he ended up reporting on the near land robbery of gargantuan proportions that had been sanctioned ten years earlier by the Statehood Act.

Wallace had tried to fly to Barrow, but the plane was fogged out and diverted to Kotzebue, where someone told him to look me up. I had just returned from the legislative session in Juneau, and he found me at my little tarpaper house in town.

I told Wallace all about the legal basis of our land claims, and explained why a settlement was essential—both to Alaska Natives and to the state itself. He wanted to visit an ordinary family in town to find out what they had to say about all this, and I suggested Elmer and Laura Davis, two Iñupiat elders who lived behind my one-room house. They were traditional people who had not been schooled in the Western sense, and I thought they perfectly represented the necessity of preserving our land.

Elmer and Laura had moved to Kotzebue from Selawik. They had a large family, and Elmer had built a shelter out of plywood, fabric, and any other materials he could find that might help keep out the cold. I entered the dim little house and asked if he would be willing to have Mike Wallace and his cameraman come in for an interview. Elmer and Laura, who were just sitting down to lunch, agreed. They put aside their midday meal of dried caribou meat and seal oil, spread out on a small table in the main room. And somewhat to my surprise, even in their broken English, they turned out to be quite eloquent.

The lens flicked open and Mike Wallace gently asked Laura who owned the cobbled-together house they lived in.

"I—he does," she said, looking at Elmer.

"Elmer, do you own this house?" Wallace asked.

"Yes, we do," Elmer replied.

"Do you own the land?"

"Yes," said Elmer.

"Do you have a piece of paper that says you own it?"

"No," said Elmer.

In that simple exchange, Elmer had conveyed the essence of the situation confronting 100,000 Alaska Natives. We had owned and controlled the land for ten thousand years, but we had no piece of paper the rest of the world would recognize. And only Congress could resolve the issue.

Elmer and Laura Davis probably never fully understood the part they played in our struggle to secure the land of our forefathers. But when *60 Minutes* aired that program, it conveyed to 20 million American TV viewers with great clarity and power just what it was we were seeking. It was an incalculably important moment for our cause.

Years later, in 2005, I walked into Senator Ted Stevens's office at the U.S. Capitol and began to gaze at the pictures on the wall. To my surprise, there, in the center of a group of Alaskan scenes, was a beautiful color picture of Elmer and Laura Davis, now long gone. Seeing Elmer and Laura promptly brought back memories of how my uneducated but warm and wise neighbors helped me to get our land claims message across to the American people when we needed it most.

17

Nanıqaqtugut!: We Have Light!

When I returned home in 1966, not much had changed from ten years before. When the midnight sun began to fade at the end of summer and darkness enveloped the Arctic world, in ten thousand small homes scattered the length and breadth of Alaska's rivers and coasts, a family member poured gasoline into the Coleman lamp and lit a match. If the Coleman lamp wasn't working, they pulled out a kerosene lamp or lit some candles.

I can't count the number of hours, day after day, month after month, year after year, that my mother Naungaġiaq sat on her caribou-skin *qaatchiaq* painstakingly working in the dim light in the years before electricity. She sewed skins for mittens, parkas, mukluks, and sealskin pants. She sat in the same place knitting socks and gloves and wristlets or making the intricate beaded designs for slippers and mukluks and fancy work for parkas. How the women kept their eyesight during those years is beyond me. And it wasn't much differ-

With Dick Miller (*top*), in 1953. Dick was a young Baptist missionary who had come to Kotzebue from Mississippi. In 1956, he arranged for me to travel Outside for high school. Here I am (*bottom*), with Auleniq, Nauṅġaġiaq, Saigulik, and little Beverly, about to fly off to boarding school in Tennessee. I was fifteen, my luggage consisted of a paper shopping bag from N. G. Hanson Trading Company, and I clearly had no idea how to dress like an American teenager!

To Brother Willie

Love Fran.

With my sister, Saigulik, and our half brothers Kermit and Jim, taken at the Kotzebue airport around 1954. This is the only picture we have of the four of us together, as Kermit and Jim were born and raised in Fairbanks (in between stints at federal boarding schools), and we rarely saw them. Frances and I had heard that Jim and Kermit were on their way to Noorvik to spend the summer with our uncle Clarence (Ipiiliik, our mother's brother), so we went to the airport to see them. Kermit was killed in Vietnam, Jim lives in Anchorage with his family, and Saigulik passed away from liver disease in the 1960s.

Me and a frozen sheefish in Kotzebue. 1953.

TOP: When I arrived for high school at Chilhowee Academy in Tennessee, I had no conception of American football. I'd never played the game before, but after growing up in Alaska, I was strong—and very fast. I played left halfback. 1958.

BOTTOM: Can you believe this was the first time I ever sat on a horse? I was visiting my senior-class girlfriend, Linda Holdman, at her home near Memphis, and she let me ride her family's Tennessee Walking Horse. 1960.

ABOVE: At camp in Ikkattuq with Nauṅġaġiaq, shortly before she died. 1966.

BELOW: With Aline Strutz, my wife Abbe's grandmother. She was an Alaska pioneer who moved here in 1920. This photo was taken during my 1974 congressional race.

TOP: Hanging out with fellow Native classmates from the University of Alaska Fairbanks during the short time I was an undergraduate student there. I was perpetually broke and behind on schoolwork—being the first person in my family to attend college, I didn't have anyone to turn to for guidance on how to make it through this strange new experience. 1960.

BOTTOM: Willie Hensley, state senator. Juneau, 1973.

TOP: "The Big Squeeze." Standing between Walter J. Hickel, then the governor of Alaska, and Ted Stevens, then a member of the Alaska House of Representatives. The photo was taken in 1969, the year Hickel took office and found himself faced with extensive Native claims to land that the state thought it was going to get under the Alaska Statehood Act.

BOTTOM LEFT: With Secretary of the Interior Stewart Udall. Without Udall's 1968 decision on the land freeze, our efforts to secure Native Alaskan lands would have been fruitless.

BOTTOM RIGHT: With State Senator Terry Miller (R-North Pole). 1972.

ABOVE: An Alaska Federation of Natives board meeting, shortly before the 1971 passage of the Alaska Native Claims Settlement Act. Etok (Charlie Edwardsen of Barrow) stands behind me. Etok and I would split over the Iñuit Circumpolar Council constitution. Here, though, we were united in our goal.

RIGHT: Before my family's last *ivrulik* (sod house) as it sinks back into the tundra at Ikkattuq. The *ivrulik* had been the home of the Iñupiat for a good ten thousand years.

Finally able to relax and spend time with my family, even as the massive ash cloud from St. Augustine's eruption looms behind! From left: James, Priscilla, Mollie, me, Elizabeth, and Abbe. 1992.

ent for the men—especially the ivory carvers, with their intricate designs and tiny lifelike reproductions of auklets, geese, dogs, bears, seals, walrus, and other animals. Vision was so important to us. But for generations, light was inadequate—especially in the Far North, where the winter sun never rises.

Electricity had come to towns like Kotzebue in the 1950s. All of a sudden we no longer needed to burn diesel oil in coffee cans out on the ice runway at night so the pilots would know where to land. We could buy freezers to preserve food instead of storing it deep in the frozen ground. Streetlights lit our way on stormy evenings. Children could advance at school because they could study at night.

Out in the villages, though, it was an entirely different story. In some, there were federal compounds where the Bureau of Indian Affairs school and the teachers' quarters had their own generators, but the rest of the village, home to 200 to 500 people, remained in the dark.

Nothing was going to help more to ease us into the twentieth century than electrifying the villages. But who was going to pay for it? How was it to happen, given the fact that the people in the villages still functioned in an almost-cashless barter economy? Being good at letter writing, I wrote some on the subject to a few people in power who might be able to help. To my surprise, Edward Lewis "Bob" Bartlett—Alaska's first U.S. senator—responded, informing me that there was a federal study under way on the feasibility of building power plants in Alaska's villages. Before long I was invited to serve on the organizing board of what turned out to be the Alaska Village Electric Cooperative (AVEC). Walter Hickel, the Republican governor of Alaska, had won his seat in the same election that sent me to Juneau. The feds agreed that he could name a majority of the AVEC board, and not surprisingly, he appointed mostly Republicans. But even with the governor's people predominating, they elected me president of AVEC and we set to work on getting the project off the ground.

The major challenge was to secure the funding. What we proposed was that the federal Office of Economic Opportunity would provide the administrative funding during the initial years of the program, using $5 million in loans from the Rural Electrification Administration for construction. But the REA, which was proud of the very low default rate on its loans, was afraid to agree to this arrangement. Agency officials had taken a look at the income levels in the villages and were shocked; they feared that Alaska's Natives wouldn't be able to afford even the guaranteed maximum twenty dollars per month they would be charged for electricity.

The best shot at changing minds at the REA was at the annual convention of the National Rural Electric Cooperative Association being held in Atlantic City, New Jersey. There, I gave a rip-roaring speech about how the REA was founded exactly for the benefit of areas like rural Alaska. It is 1969, I said, and without electricity, we would be frozen in time. I conceded that it was a novel idea to try to run a statewide utility in the largest state in the union from a central location, with maintenance workers traveling to the villages. But the Native people were honest, I declared, and would pay their bills even though the managers' office was five hundred miles away.

It worked. After we met with agency leaders in Washington, the REA committed the money and we were on our way. We had a very limited budget for labor in each village, but interestingly, in the first ten we selected for power, the villagers essentially volunteered to help build the plants. It was that important, in their view, for them to have electricity to help them in their daily lives.

Our board of directors met many times throughout the initial years to plan for operations, operator training, and maintenance. We had to secure commitments from both state and federal schools. And we had to persuade the Bureau of Indian Affairs to shut down the generators that had always powered the BIA's own facilities and to buy power from AVEC instead. In the end, we managed to create a statewide power entity that has successfully provided power for fifty of the largest villages throughout the state. (Many of the other approximately 150 villages now generate power independently.)

Like other modern conveniences, including heat and indoor plumbing, electricity became a change agent in the villages. For people who have always had power, being able to flip on a switch to provide light seems inconsequential. It is something they do without a thought—until the power goes out and their world falls apart. For those who have never had power, electricity is almost a miracle, providing the basis for a host of physical improvements that come later: indoor hot water and sewer systems, new schools, airport facilities, medical clinics, streetlights, and Laundromats. Without electricity, these are all impossible.

The price of this valuable new resource was a recurring bill that came in the mail every month—something that was entirely new to village life. We had never had mortgages or utility bills. What we bought, we had paid for in barter or with small amounts of cash. The big question among the Washington policymakers had been whether the Natives would pay their newfound bills to a faceless entity hundreds of miles away when cash was scarce. They did and they do, to this day.

That said, paying these bills is becoming a major challenge. The cost of fuel for these far-flung power plants is prohibitively expensive—in fact, stratospheric. As I write, soaring oil prices are pushing the delivered cost of heating oil toward eight dollars a gallon, including storage, and that cost may climb higher. Few families can afford it anymore without making major sacrifices in some other aspect of their lives, despite a special state fund established to subsidize the cost of electricity.

The Iñuit have a long and complicated history with oil—*uqsruq*. A thousand generations of our forefathers powered their bodies and fed their dogs and kept the *iglus* warm with seal oil, whale oil, and walrus oil. Seal oil practically runs in our veins, since we use it to store everything from roots to blubber and you cannot eat an Eskimo meal without it. And we have a long and complicated history with Outsiders who prized the oil.

It was the demand for fuel that originally lured Europeans to Greenland. In just a few hundred years, the whales were virtually wiped out in that part of the world. Similarly, American whalers from New England chased the whales in hunts that could last three or four years from the Atlantic to the Pacific and on up to the Arctic Ocean. After many years of winter hunting in Hawaii, the whalers learned to literally freeze their ships in the shallow, safer waters of the Arctic so that they could be there, waiting, when the whales ended their annual migration in the spring. By the late 1800s, the whaling ships had almost killed off both the whale and the walrus populations, causing widespread starvation in Alaska's coastal communities.

As the Yankee whalers embedded themselves in the Arctic, the Iñuit whalers themselves became prized hunters for the white men. Their fortunes rose with the price of baleen (or "whalebone," as it was often called when used in corsets and collar stays). Then, in 1865, with the discovery of crude oil in Pennsylvania, whaling fell into a steep decline—as did the economy of the Iñuit. But the whales, thankfully, had an opportunity to go forth and multiply, restoring their numbers.

When I was ten years old, I somehow got the duty of filling a small canvas bag with sand and gravel from the beach in Kotzebue and mailing it to the Shell Oil Company. Apparently their geologists wanted to see if there was some prospect for petroleum development in the region. But the big discovery came much later. For millennia, the Iñuit had been aware of oil seeps in the North Slope of Alaska, and used them for their own fuel. But it was only in 1968 that explorers for Atlantic Richfield discovered over 10 billion barrels of crude oil lying below the surface at Prudhoe Bay.

The discovery came in the midst of our battle for Native rights to traditional lands, and for us, it meant both new problems and new opportunities. At first the oil industry— along with most everyone else—seemed to expect Alaska's Natives to remain complacent as their exploitation of this mighty newfound resource proceeded. That's what we'd done when the missionaries Christianized us, and when the Constitutional Convention made Alaska a state without any consideration for its Native population. But we weren't going to be so easy this time. And ultimately—new proof that politics makes strange bedfellows—that meant that the oil industry was forced to become an ally in our land claims battle, because until the land claims were settled and clear title was established, no development could take place.

Later, Alaska's Natives actively supported the construction of the Trans-Alaska Pipeline. We knew that without it, and without the revenues that would flow from the project to the state's coffers, Alaska could never provide the schools, housing, electricity, airports, and other facilities we so badly needed. I personally believe that if the oil companies had not been able to find, pump, transport, and sell the oil under Prudhoe Bay, Alaska might have had to rescind statehood. There simply was no other way a state government ever could have been viable. The population would have remained tiny and taxes would have been so astronomical that no one could have afforded to live there.

The very notion of statehood had been based on a premise that the new state would be able to survive on what could be developed out of the 104 million acres transferred to it from the federal government. And the state was also to get 90 percent of all revenues from activities—such as oil leasing, logging, and mining—on the remaining federal land. Without all that, it was clear to me, there could be no state.

Over the years, we have often been at loggerheads with America's environmental movement. Environmentalists bitterly opposed the Trans-Alaska Pipeline, for example. And in the late 1970s, they wholeheartedly supported a Carter administration initiative to "Save the Whales" and end whaling. But whaling is an integral part of Iñuit heritage, and to this day, the source of a vital food staple in many Alaskan coastal villages. As time has passed, the environmental community has come to understand the nature of the Alaska Native's interaction with the natural universe, and most often supports the hunting and fishing economy that is integral to our communities.

But back then, understanding was in short supply. The Iñuit fought fiercely against the Carter policy. They began a lengthy campaign to show that scientists were using flawed methodology to measure the population of whales, and they became regular visitors to the meetings of the International Whaling Commission, arguing forcefully for their right to hunt whales for community use—as opposed to commercial use. In time, they worked out accommodations with the IWC, and today, the Iñuit continue to hunt whales under its guidelines.

The Iñuit and other Alaska Natives cannot afford to be purists in their views on the environment. We have had to be pragmatic, to judge what is in our best interests. Our perspective on nature is multidimensional, and this is not an easy concept for many activist environmentalists to grasp.

We are very conscious of the fact that most Americans no longer live in pristine areas, and that the wild and open country that once was America is no longer. We also know that most people never see the blood spilling, the feathers flying, the guts and skin being harvested, as an animal dies so that people may have protein. All they see is a nice little package wrapped in plastic. By contrast, for Alaska Natives, the whole process is something we are engaged in on a daily basis. All parts of the animal are valuable to us—skins and tusks and hoofs and intestines and stomachs—for a variety of purposes.

No precious resource goes to waste in our world, least of all the oil, whatever its source, that has nourished us, warmed us, and lit our way for thousands of years. It continues to do so today—a fact that modern technology has made beautifully visible. In nighttime photographs of Earth from outer space, you see the cities of the world bathed in light, strung like pearls along stretches of river and ocean and highway. If you focus on Alaska, the villages are almost invisible. But look closely, and there they are, tiny footprints of light.

18

Atautchıkuaq: As One

I would fly anywhere, talk to anyone, to get our message out. In 1969, I was invited to a conference in Le Havre, France, that was organized by Professor Jean Malaurie, the head of the Fondation Française d'Etudes Nordiques. He had amassed roughly one hundred experts from Europe and North America—economists, academics, anthropologists, and others—to address Iñuit affairs. Among the gathering were a few Iñuit leaders from North America and Greenland.

It was a rare Alaskan Iñuk who had ever met anyone from Greenland, even though our people have common origins, language, and culture, having spread out from Alaska several thousand years ago. But despite all the time that had elapsed since our forefathers shared the same space many millennia ago, despite the great distances we had traveled apart, for me, it was like meeting the neighbor next door. There was an instantaneous connection among us, a spark of celebration, recognition, and understanding. Despite thousands of years of separation, we were connected by our culture and history. We even had much of our language in common.

There were real differences, of course. Greenland had been colonized by the Danes in the eighteenth century, and its people had inevitably been profoundly influenced by Danish language and culture—and by being part of Europe. The Greenlanders I met in France made me feel a bit like a country bumpkin. They seemed so cosmopolitan, and they tended to be fluent in several languages. I was much impressed by Angmalortoq Olsen, a tall, handsome Iñuk with wavy hair who lived in Copenhagen. And the Greenlanders were also more politically sophisticated. We Alaskans, for example, still had a tendency to operate through consensus. The Greenland Iñuit, by contrast, were quite comfortable with the tough give-and-take of opposition-party politics. In fact, two of the men I met during that trip—Lars Chemnitz and Jonathan Motzfeldt—became prime ministers of Greenland years later, after Denmark granted Greenland home rule. But despite such differences, I became deeply conscious of our common roots. The Greenlanders' greatest concern at this time was a battle to preserve their language in the face of great pressures to make Danish the primary language in the schools and in government.

I told the gathering how, despite millennia of occupying Alaska's 375 million acres, we had fee title to only 500 acres. I explained how the Statehood Act had created a built-in conflict with our aboriginal title that only the U.S. Congress could resolve. I said: "We are testing the American political system. We have found it responsive up to this time and have hope. We know the history of our country in dealing with the American Indian and want to see a final chapter not written in blood or in deception or in injustice. We are seeking an al-

ternative to wardship. . . . We want to be able to live longer
and more decently without having to stoop in indignity because of a degrading welfare system." If we failed to win a
fair settlement, I warned, "America will have lost an opportunity to right old wrongs and for once allow the first American a fair deal."

The committee of "experts" on Native peoples who met
after the conference did not include our land settlement as
one of their nine recommendations. They represented the
typical non-Native paternalistic system that had long been in
operation in Europe. They owed their positions to their governments and they could not see that we sought to stand on
our own two feet as we had done for thousands of years. But
they provided a needed forum for our views, and the experience reinforced our understanding of what a huge challenge
lay before us.

Back in the United States, we were beginning to amass a var-
ied group of supporters. We were also winning over some
disbelievers. Congressman Wayne Aspinall, a Colorado Democrat, was chairman of the House Interior and Insular Affairs
Committee, which had considerable jurisdiction over issues
that mattered to us. In the summer of 1966, I asked permission to appear before a special committee Congress had created called the Public Land Law Review Commission. As
chairman, Aspinall at first turned me down. They were dealing only with "public lands," he said. I gave him my usual
reply: there were no public lands in Alaska—nothing but Native lands. Eventually Congressman Aspinall changed his
mind and allowed me to testify at their hearing in Anchorage. It was the first time a formal body listened to my ideas
about who owned Alaska, and in the end, Aspinall himself

came around. He went further than I ever could have imagined, ultimately declaring, on the floor of the House of Representatives, that "forty million acres is not enough for these people!"

Richard Nixon, it was said, had known only one Native American—a football coach at Whittier College in California when Nixon was a student—and had greatly admired the man. Had he not been an Indian, Nixon felt, he might have coached at a Big Ten school. Several White House aides, including John Ehrlichman, one of the president's closest counselors, were acutely aware that Nixon had gotten excellent press for his support of New Mexico's Taos Pueblo Indians in their fight to reclaim traditional religious lands. Perhaps they saw a similar popularity-boosting opportunity in our land claims.

Whatever the reason, we found unexpected sympathy in Nixon's administration. I have always been amused by the irony: it was, after all, Mr. Nixon's Quaker forefathers from Whittier, California, whose missionaries had come to "save souls" in my part of Alaska and worked so hard to suppress our language, change our customs, alienate our children, and generally cut our people off from our cultural roots.

Nixon's vice president, Spiro Agnew, was another unlikely ally. In 1967, President Lyndon Johnson had appointed me as the first Alaska Native to sit on the National Council on Indian Opportunity, a body he had created to focus on poverty and other issues confronting American Indians. After Nixon was elected, Agnew inherited the chairmanship of the council, whose members included Donald Rumsfeld, then the head of the Office of Economic Opportunity, and George Shultz, the secretary of labor.

This was an incredible opportunity to spread our message. At least six members of the president's cabinet attended each meeting—people who could be powerful advocates of any cause. Every time I had a chance to speak to the cabinet members and the vice president, my goal was to press for support for our Native land claims. Appropriately enough, our meetings took place in the Indian Treaty Room in the Old Executive Office Building. God only knows how many millions of acres of Indian land had been taken by hook or by crook in this very room over the course of two hundred years. I just hoped that Alaska Natives were not going to join the ranks of tribes who had given up land for blankets or a few cents an acre and been relegated to reservations that constituted only a fraction of their former holdings.

Partly as a result of the contacts we made in that council, the Nixon administration eventually backed our quest for a settlement. One person key to Nixon's support was Bobbie Greene Kilberg, a youthful Yale graduate who had worked on the New Mexico Taos Pueblo legislation that had won the president such good press. Kilberg, along with domestic policy adviser Leonard Garment and his assistant, Brad Patterson, helped keep the Alaska Native claims legislation at the forefront of Nixon's domestic policy agenda.

Slowly, the momentum was building. At home, our old ally Bill Egan was reelected governor in 1970—a great help to us because of his ability to work with the Democrats who controlled the congressional committees. Democrat Nick Begich, once my roommate in Juneau, became Alaska's lone congressman, a force to be reckoned with on the House Interior and Insular Affairs Committee.

Newspaper editorials, church groups, and civil rights organizations went on record supporting our cause. And in the meantime, the oil companies finally began to see the light. Our land claims had stymied state land selections—and along with them, the creation of the corridor destined for the 800-mile-long Trans-Alaska Pipeline—and the consortium of oil companies slated to build the pipeline wanted the problem solved as quickly as possible. Ultimately they joined in the effort to pass a "fair" Native claims settlement bill. The environmental community also recognized an opportunity to preserve millions of acres for public enjoyment. Although they had little interest in Natives, they saw that in supporting us, they could also push their own agenda. The Alaskan business community realized, at long last, that the legal system was not going to quash the Alaska Natives' claims, and gave up the fight against us. And we worked hard to heal schisms within the Native power structure by carefully accommodating the special needs of certain regions. By taking into account Native groups large and small, who spoke different languages, came from different historical backgrounds, and were spread over an area two and a half times the size of Texas, we attempted to craft a settlement that would be fair to all, focusing on just allotment and redistribution of lands and funds.

All of these developments, combined with the positive intervention of President Nixon in the spring of 1971, led to an increasingly affirmative environment on Capitol Hill. And over the next five months, both the Senate and the House of Representatives passed versions of the Alaska Native Claims Settlement Act. The battle was not over: as a conference committee worked to reconcile the two bills, the system worked to minimize the size of the settlement.

In the end, a bill was passed and signed into law by President Nixon. It awarded Alaska Natives 44 million acres of land—about 16 percent of Alaska's territory—and $962.5 million for relinquishing claims to the rest. To administer the land and the money, the act called for the establishment of a system of village and regional corporations whose shareholders would be eligible Alaska Natives.

We had begun, five years before, with Alaska Natives having no recognized claim over any of our traditional lands. Now we had nearly $1 billion and 44 million acres of land, deeded to us by the highest authorities in the land. It had taken sacrifice, energy, and commitment from all of Alaska's tribes. Not everyone was happy with the outcome; there were those who felt strongly that we should have held out for more. But when the Alaska Federation of Natives voted on the settlement, before President Nixon signed it into law, the result was 511 delegates in favor, 56 against. For better or worse, we had won.

19

Tuvaaqatiga: My Companion

When my first marriage ended, just as my years of fighting for Native rights was finally yielding success, I was lonely and disconnected, and for the first time in my life, I felt like a failure. I had been unsuccessful at something that seemed so easy for everyone else. In the summer of 1971, months before the final land settlement bill was passed into law, I retreated to Kotzebue, and in retrospect, I can see that I was deeply depressed. I didn't know enough to see a shrink. I didn't know anyone who saw one. I didn't even know one. I was on my own.

My self-prescribed therapy was to write poetry. I had never done so before, but it seemed somehow like the only way I could prove to myself that I was still alive and connected to the earth. One poem was inspired by a little confrontation I had, after passage of the Land Claims Act, with a *naluaġmiut* lady friend in Kotzebue who said she was beginning to feel like a member of a minority—and also by the sight of some neighbor women trudging up the beach road, pushing against the wind in their colorful calico parkas. I called it "Change":

In Kotzebue today
we feel the fear
of change

Dark eyes dart
quickly forward
to meet the new

Challenges combine
as once before
in days of sod and snow
no armor stood before
the naked Eskimo
as cannon boomed
and prayers combined
to mold
a cold philosophy

Now anxious azure eyes
implore the remnant tribe
to feel the fear he felt before
but now reverse the role

Impossible to turn the clock,
to rock about among the dogs
whose litter threatens exodus
from lonely Arctic winds

The winds abate
leaving frozen forms of sadness
deep crevasses
etched upon the parchment
aged by time

Hooded figures bend
Before the brewing breeze
as gentle lapping waves
caress the ancient shores
of Kotzebue

These attempts at creativity made me feel alive again, and just being in Kotzebue helped me regain my footing. Once I got back to Juneau, it was not long before I met Abigale Ryan, who worked for one of my friends, Senator George Hohman, from Bethel, Alaska. She had a wonderful smile, would laugh at my jokes, and didn't treat me as if I were an alien, unlike most people who thought of me as a shiftless rabble-rouser. And I liked her dog, Zak. We were the perfect trio.

Abbe's maternal grandparents, Aline and Louis Strutz, are considered Alaska pioneers. They had met at Fort George Wright in Washington State. Aline was from Montana. Louis was sent to Alaska by the military in 1919, and Aline joined him the following year. They were married, and Louis went to work for the Engineering Commission, precursor of the Alaska Railroad.

Abbe's mother, Gayle, was one of their six children. She was working at Emard's Cannery, down at the mouth of Ship Creek, when she met James Ryan, Abbe's father. There were three other daughters at home, and in those days, the young men of the bustling little city of Anchorage came to visit the Strutz family in swarms. Among the young suitors was a friend of James Ryan's, Walter Hickel, who was stuck on Gayle's younger sister Ermalee. Wally was dyslexic, energetic, and pugnacious. He was from Kansas, the son of a tenant farmer. He had arrived in Alaska in 1940, with just thirty-seven cents in his pocket.

James Ryan became a plumber and pipe fitter. After he and Gayle married, the family followed the custom of the day, motoring to Alaska for the summer construction season and heading back south when the first snow—"termination dust"—fell on the Chugach Mountains behind Anchorage. They bought an old stone house in Oroville, California, north of Sacramento, where James kept a few cows. There was a small orchard with orange, lemon, and grapefruit trees, grapes, and a plethora of flowers. It was like a little Garden of Eden.

Meanwhile, Wally Hickel married Ermalee Strutz and became a construction magnate and hotel owner, as well as a statehood booster and active Republican. He was elected governor in 1966 by a slim margin, just as our Native land claims movement was gathering steam. And after the discovery of oil at Prudhoe Bay in 1968, he had to face the claims issue head-on. His initial approach—a strenuous effort to crush our claims, since he hoped to use the oil resources to balance the paltry state checkbook—was seared into my memory. So I was stunned to learn, after Abbe and I began to date in Juneau, that she was related to the Hickels. But Abbe's father was a dyed-in-the-wool Democrat. I figured that if he could deal with that business-labor nexus, so could I. Before long I asked Abbe to marry me.

I had now been in the state legislature for nearly eight years, and I knew all too well how difficult it was to have a normal life on a lawmaker's salary. While it seemed pretty normal to me to live hand-to-mouth, it was not normal for Abbe. So in 1974, partly because it would allow me to take a new direction in life and partly just because I thought I could win, I decided to run for Congress, for the seat held by my friend Don Young. Don had won a special election in 1973 after the untimely death of Congressman Nick Begich, who had disappeared in a small plane with House majority leader Hale Boggs, the father of broadcast journalist Cokie Roberts, on a flight from Anchorage to Juneau.

My congressional campaign was a shoestring operation, to say the least. I had two employees—a campaign manager, Karen Hedlund, and a speechwriter and all-around aide, Gordon Parker. We were having the time of our lives, working hard to win the primary against John Havelock, who had been Alaska's attorney general under Governor Bill Egan, and looking forward to the fall campaign against the incumbent. It was one of the few times ever that an Alaska Native had run head-on against a non-Native in a statewide election.

As the Fourth of July approached, we decided that I should go to the small city of Seward, which had a tradition of whooping it up big-time, with a parade and an annual footrace up Mount Marathon, drawing big crowds. Seward is in southern Alaska, set against a stunning backdrop of mountains and fjords. I woke up early that day and headed to the train station to join Gordon. The train was filled with revelers from engine to caboose, we had a film crew on board that was going to start work on my television ads, and we had arranged for a welcoming demonstration in Seward.

For me, this was new territory. In my rural village district we campaigned, but not too aggressively. But in urban politics, I was discovering that you couldn't be shy. You had to get out there and tout your accomplishments, using the word "I" a lot. I had been raised to believe that you let your accomplishments speak for themselves and that people would elect you if they felt your heart was in the right place. But I was determined to do this. So I campaigned my buns off. We shook every hand on the train, giving out buttons, and my film crew whirred away the whole time.

As we neared Seward, I could see my clutch of supporters holding up HENSLEY FOR CONGRESS signs. I got off the train with my little entourage and eagerly headed for the crowds. It was going to be a glorious day. I could feel it in my bones.

On the way to the main street where all the celebrants were gathering, a two-man log-sawing contest was taking place. It's never hard to get my competitive instincts going, so one of my supporters grabbed one end of the saw and the two of us started cutting the two-foot-thick log. The sun was really beating down, and I was sweltering by the time we finished, terribly in need of liquid. Someone offered me some wine, and I took a couple of swigs. Big mistake!

I started walking toward Main Street to shake hands and join the parade. But all of a sudden the horizon started tilting and my head began to pound. I had developed an instant hangover. I had to run for an alley, where I vomited. My head was still pounding and I knew I needed to get back to normal as quickly as possible to continue the campaign.

I had seen people with hangovers take a drink in the morning to cure themselves, and thought maybe that would work. So I slipped into a bar, empty except for a couple of tourists, and ordered a vodka and tonic. It didn't help. I kept having to run for the bathroom. Then I just sat for a while in the dim light, and finally I began to feel better. I headed back outside to do my duty with the voters. As I stepped out into the sun, Gordon Parker ran up to me.

"Where the hell have you been?" he demanded. "We have a crisis on our hands!"

Then he sputtered out that my friend John Shively had called the Seward police to say that he was speeding toward Providence Hospital in Anchorage with Abbe, who was about to deliver our first child, and she wanted me there. The police had called Mayor Lee McInerney on the Fourth of July parade grounds, and she had made an announcement on the loudspeaker: "If anyone knows the whereabouts of Willie Hensley, his wife is having a baby!"

The announcement had been met with wild cheers, even though I was nowhere to be found.

Gordon and I frantically called around and finally found a sober pilot, who flew me back to Anchorage, landing a float-plane with pontoons on Lake Hood. From there, I dashed to the hospital, and an hour and a half later, Priscilla Naunġaġiaq Aline Hensley was born.

Priscilla was going to carry on the name and spirit of two wonderful people, Naunġaġiaq, an Iñupiaq born on the dog-team trail, and Aline Strutz, a pioneer Alaskan who had arrived in Anchorage when it was not much more than a tent city. Two years later, following a wild ride through at least two red lights to the Alaska Native Hospital, Mary Lynn— Mollie—was born. I gave her the name Aurvik, after Naunġaġiaq's older sister. Three years after Mollie came James, whom I named Umiivik, in honor of the husband of Siichiaq, the childless woman who adopted Naunġaġiaq and probably saved her life. Our last child I named in honor of my sister Saigulik—Frances. Elizabeth Frances Saigulik Hensley emerged with a thatch of hair as black as mine, a stark contrast to the red hair of her sisters. I always tell people that is because I gave it everything I had at the end.

Back on the Fourth of July in 1974, Priscilla's birth and the drama of getting me there turned out to be one of the high points of my campaign for Congress. The next day, the *Anchorage Times* carried a front-page story, complete with a picture of me holding Priscilla and Abbe looking over my shoulder.

I went on to win the primary election against John Havelock, and Don Young and I faced off in a good, clean campaign, quite different from the politics of personal destruction that is so common today. By November, the race was very close. I even heard that Don was filling out a résumé, thinking that his time in Congress was up. But as it turned out, I won only 44 percent of the vote and Don went back to Washington, where he has now served eighteen straight terms in the House of Representatives. He became chairman of the House Resources Committee and later the House Committee on Transportation and Infrastructure. As I write, he is running for his nineteenth term in office.

To this day, Don Young and his wife, Lu, are good friends of mine. And in retrospect, I am glad he won. I loved politics, and I love that in the United States, virtually anyone with the interest and the drive can participate. But I discovered that holding office does not define who you are. Being defeated was probably one of the best things that ever happened to me. I was able to move on to accomplish other things I never thought I had the talent to do.

20

Manıgnıt Aŋalatchırugut: We Become Businessmen

The Native Claims Settlement Act had created one dozen regional and 226 village corporations, all of them wholly owned by shareholding Native Alaskans. The regional corporations' boundaries were drawn roughly along traditional ethnic lines. Doyon Ltd., for example, represented the Athapascans in the state's interior, and the Sealaska Corporation represented the Tlingit and Haida tribes in the southeast. NANA Regional Corporation, an outgrowth of the Northwest Alaska Native Association, represented Kotzebue and the other Iñuit villages in the region where I was born and raised.

My land claims research in 1966 had made me acutely aware of the fact that Native people in general had not had any real function in the economy other than as consumers or laborers or as human magnets for federal funding. We lived at a subsistence level, supplementing our traditional sources of sustenance with whatever cash we could earn from fur trapping, fishing, and summer jobs. We generally had little contact with banks and almost no experience with the financial world. In fact, when I got my first mortgage in 1975, I thought it meant I had to live in the house for thirty years!

Before 1971, at least in the Arctic, we pretty much owed our soul to the company store. Traders had the goods and we paid whatever price they asked for what we needed. They would permit our families to live on credit most of the winter as long as we made occasional payments and didn't go over a set limit. By the time I became aware of business and trade, this arrangement had been in place for half a century.

Now, suddenly, all that had changed. Congress had determined that every qualified Alaska Native born prior to December 18, 1971, would own one hundred shares of stock in a village and a regional corporation. As a result, the Native Alaskans were thrust directly and abruptly into the mainstream of American corporate life. And as we had so many times in the past, the Native people began the process of adapting to the new order and figuring out how to make the new arrangement work for us.

Years later, one Tlingit leader compared the emergence of the Native corporations to being born adult, and then having to learn to walk and talk. It is amazing how much we learned to do in a very short time. Starting from the barest of beginnings, we had to comprehend the very nature of business and to understand the responsibilities we had as directors, officers, and shareholders of the corporations. We had to master the day-to-day work of strategizing, coming up with ideas, implementing and managing them. Along the way, we had to learn about matters that had never before concerned our people: depreciation, life-estate stock, foreign currency fluctuations. But we did it. And before too long, the fruits of our labor began to be visible. We started businesses—hotels, construction, food service, and insurance companies—that would employ our shareholders.

Each of the Native corporations invested its capital in different ways, with differing levels of success. Sealaska Corporation, with headquarters in Juneau, put its money into a wide range of ventures, from forest products to plastics, and was the first Native corporation to make the Fortune 500 list. The Cook Inlet Region, Inc., prospered in an entirely different way. Under the terms of the settlement act, CIRI was entitled to nearly 800,000 acres of land, but Anchorage dominated the region, and the rest was mountaintops and glaciers, leaving little productive land for the corporation to develop. Ultimately, CIRI won the right to choose federal surplus lands anywhere in the United States, and its leaders invested in real estate and other ventures far from home.

The Arctic Slope Regional Corporation was in a unique position. Its territory—5 million acres on Alaska's North Slope—encompassed the rich oil fields of Prudhoe Bay. In the mid-1960s, Iñupiat leaders in Barrow, the region's largest village, had provided energy and manpower to the Alaska Federation of Natives as we pursued a land settlement. After protracted political and legal battles, they succeeded in establishing the North Slope Borough, America's largest municipality, incorporating 89,000 square miles of Arctic territory. In so doing, they had the legal authority to force the oil industry to accept Iñupiat control over all drilling operations in the area, and they reaped tax revenues from the billions of dollars of investments in infrastructure: worker accommodations, warehouses, production facilities, and pipeline.

At NANA, we started out with about 4,800 shareholders and were to select 2.2 million acres of land. Our share of the settlement money came to about $50 million. Without hesitation, we set about bringing our new corporation to life. We selected a board of directors, officers, and a president. Our people began to hold annual meetings, usually in Iñupiaq and English. They learned about cumulative voting, dividends, and balance sheets. For the first time, we were the leaders of an entity of our own that controlled significant amounts of capital and land. We did not have to ask a representative of Uncle Sam for permission to act. We were floating on an unknown sea on a vessel none of us really knew how to captain toward a destination impossible to imagine.

In the beginning, we had little idea what a corporation was or what it could become. But we put our spirit, goodwill, and communal effort into designing NANA's structure, adding some important elements of our traditional approach to getting things done. Our past livelihood had always depended upon the recognition that achieving success required the effort of all our people, so the corporation we created was not a typically hierarchical arrangement. There were checks and balances, and ways of recognizing special talents. Those who had good Iñupiaq language skills ratcheted up in importance and became a bridge to the older generation and more traditional people. Those well versed in *naluaġmiut* knowledge— accounting and finance, for instance—did the grunt work of corporate bureaucracy.

We worked with the Alaska Federation of Natives and lobbied Congress to make sure that only land that had been developed could be taxed; undeveloped land would remain just that—to be used as our people had used it for untold generations. We also created an Elders Council, made up of some of our most prestigious village leaders, whose mission was to advise us on potentially contentious issues. When we decided to develop the Red Dog Mine about ninety miles

north of Kotzebue—the largest zinc deposit in the world—
we had to face its inevitable impact on the migration of the
caribou. With the help of the Elders Council, we consulted
with our people and came to a consensus that the jobs the
mine would create were well worth any effect it might have
on our caribou hunting.

During our long-fought battle for our own land, I never
doubted that Alaska Natives could manage whatever settlement we could wrest from the U.S. government. We would
use common sense, as always, and we would try to use the
settlement for the betterment of our people.

As it turned out, of course, the corporation—not the
tribe—was the vehicle Congress chose for managing Native
land and money. And like most institutions we have received
from Western civilization, this corporate setup can be a decidedly mixed blessing.

A corporation that is managed in the traditional Western
sense is expected to maximize returns to its shareholders by
generating the greatest possible profits. Shareholder returns
are a foundation of American securities laws. As a result,
managers can find themselves taking risks that skate on the
edge of propriety, even when fully legal. But in our case, we
had to maintain close contact and good relations with shareholders who were also our friends, family members, and
neighbors. They might even be part of management. The
roles and responsibilities so clearly laid out in securities law
were not so clear when applied to Native villagers.

For their part, members of the tribe also could think of
themselves narrowly as shareholders. There was a risk that
they might grow addicted to rich and frequent dividends
and expect financial rewards in perpetuity, forgetting the
broader mandate of the corporation: to preserve and nurture
its asset base, which was founded upon ancestral lands and

resources needed for future generations. Ultimately, if the corporation should become unprofitable for long enough, its shrinking net worth might threaten the very land base that was the impetus for its founding.

But the corporation does not have to run the risk of becoming a sinkhole. It can act as a fortress for guarding our spirit, identity, traditions, language, and values. It can both preserve our lands and nurture the uniqueness and continuity of our people. It just takes conscious, vigilant effort on the part of managers and shareholders alike to make sure all of this happens. That effort is essential.

At NANA, we worked as hard on developing cooperative relationships with other local entities as we did on making investments and generating profits. We took satisfaction in using our institutions to foster basic human values—cooperation, sharing, hard work, and humility, among others—that had sustained our people in another, fast-disappearing age. During my years at NANA, I often reflected on those lessons I had learned as a boy in the bush. They still applied, even in business: Know your environment. Know your partners. Plan ahead. Use only as much manpower and resources as necessary. Make sure your efforts benefit the whole community.

So much had changed, and yet the essence was the same.

By 1974 we were incorporated, staffed, focused on land selection, and in the early stages of determining what investments we should make to create jobs and earn profits. And in 1975, after losing my run for Congress, I went to work for NANA full-time, starting with NANA Environmental Systems, which I created.

From the start, we took it as a given that NANA must be

profitable, and we worked to ensure that dividends were distributed every year before Christmas. But rather than concentrate on the rate of return, we focused on investing our $50 million in ways that would allow our people to be trained and employed, yet still practice traditional pursuits. We knew that the corporation could not provide lifetime security for shareholders, but it could serve as a vehicle to help them prosper in a rapidly changing world. We invested in a hotel and local tourism business, in a Kobuk River jade mine, in seafood processing, and in the Red Dog Mine. We even invested in the reindeer business—a cautionary tale that gives some insight into how much and how fast we had to learn.

We were almost completely ignorant about reindeer, which require a lot of attention and care. We were equally ignorant about the rise in popularity of their horns. Although reindeer had originally been imported from Siberia for their meat and skin, by the time we got into the business, the horns were far more valuable than the meat. To get the meat, you had to kill the reindeer. To get the horns, you had to keep him alive, and he kept on giving, regrowing the horns.

It turned out that Koreans believed fervently that deer horn, ground up and consumed in a variety of concoctions, could elevate the libido and enhance male sexual performance, and they were willing to pay dearly for such a precious commodity. For NANA, this was a great opportunity. We hired a year-round staff to manage the reindeer and made a deal with a Korean entrepreneur in San Francisco to sell our horn for forty dollars a pound, many times the going rate. We also set up a marketing joint venture that gave us a share of profits from the finished product.

Neophytes that we were, our deer-raising techniques at first were chaotic and crazed: we used helicopters, motorcycles, snow machines, and horses and ran ourselves ragged over the tundra and tussocks, trying to get the deer into the corral so that we could clip the horns with limb-cutters, inoculate the animals for disease, and brand them. NANA had a steep learning curve, but eventually the old-time herders taught us enough about herding so that it became less of a hassle.

The Quipqiña reindeer business was the province of my nephew, John Schaeffer. Despite the fact that I am his uncle, Johnny is two years older than I am, and I admire him very much. A veteran of the army's 181st Airborne Division, he had married young and had five children almost immediately. He had built a house, commanded soldiers, jumped out of airplanes, and been in real jobs—all before I recruited him to help implement the land claims settlement in our region. That had meant organizing NANA, beginning the selection of more than 2 million acres of land, and investing the nearly $50 million in settlement funds we received—all this in an area where almost everyone lived below the poverty line and almost no one had ever run a business.

Johnny had power of attorney to have NANA manage the herd of a Nome couple named Kakaruk. The couple's million-acre reindeer range abutted that of a man named Larry Davis, a tough, respected herder originally from our region. Larry was getting ready to move his herd to a corral along the Bering seacoast east of Nome to begin cutting horn and branding fawns. But the Kakaruk reindeer had gotten mixed up with Larry's lot. My nephew had gone to court, filing a lawsuit to prevent the roundup. The judge refused to issue an injunction, but he did stipulate that it was illegal for Larry to take horn that didn't belong to him. At that point, my nephew called me in to help resolve the issue. During the controversy, Johnny had called Larry a rustler on the radio, so they weren't exactly on civil terms.

It was just the sort of challenge I loved—finding a solution to a knotty problem; I always believed it was possible to resolve conflicts. So I flew to Nome and drove out to the Davis corral. I spotted the Korean who had contracted to buy Larry's horn. I introduced myself and told him I wanted to help find a way out of the situation. As we were speaking, Larry walked toward us, sweating profusely and cussing under his breath. He marched past us without a word of greeting and ducked into his tent, and the Korean went in after him. I decided to follow—and just as I was reaching for the tent flap, I heard the Korean speak.

"Willie Hensley, with NANA, is here," he told Larry. There was a short silence.

"Tell the sons of bitches that I'll see them in court," came the angry response. I had my hand on the tent flap, ready to walk in. I wasn't sure whether I should go ahead and open the flap or run for my life.

Finally I decided to take my chances. I walked in and found Larry sitting on his haunches, having a cup of coffee and still sweating from the exertion on the tundra. He looked at me, then averted his eyes.

"Sometimes my nephew Johnny gets a little carried away," I told him.

We knew that much of the Kakaruk herd was mixed in with his, I continued. If he cut horn that did not belong to him, I warned, he could be in legal trouble according to the judge. But then I suggested a solution. NANA had a helicopter and several herders who could help Larry and his sons with the corralling, and we could set it up so that one BIA agent and one Bureau of Land Management employee would referee, deciding which horns were Larry's and which belonged to the Kakaruks. We would put them in separate piles. He could have 90 percent of the fawns in the herd—a traditional arrangement if someone else's fawns were in your range.

Larry didn't accept the offer, but he did agree not to de-horn any reindeer until he talked to his lawyer. I knew I had an opening. If it was okay, I said, I would write out a settlement agreement and get it to him.

I rushed into Nome, found an old typewriter in the de-crepit movie theater a friend of mine was operating, and wrote out the deal I had suggested. Larry bought it. The roundup took place. And God only knows how many happy Koreans back in the old country had their sexual performance enhanced thanks to our labor out on the tundra.

21

Iġġıch Isuat: The End of the Mountains

By the time we were in our late thirties and early forties, many of my friends, like me, had become businessmen and politicians, and were running corporations, municipalities, and other institutions. Even so—even though it was no longer a matter of survival—we still loved to hunt. We craved traditional food, and we loved the camaraderie of the chase. Still do. And always will.

One Labor Day weekend, on a perfectly clear September day, a gang of five of us got together to take Dennis Tiepelman's big jet boat up the Kobuk River about two hundred miles from Kotzebue. We planned to catch our winter's supply of meat as the caribou emerged from the Brooks Range, heading south for the season. We had supplies to last a week—fuel for the four-hundred-mile round-trip, tents and bedding, and cold-weather gear like parkas and gloves in the event it snowed, which occasionally happens in the summer up near the mountains. We were headed to a special spot, where we would dig, foxhole-style, giving ourselves a vantage that would go for miles up into the mountains so we could see the caribou as they meandered down from the North Slope, heading for their winter range farther south. This herd, numbering about a half million caribou, has been a source of protein and warm skins for the Iñupiat for thousands of years.

Dennis was head of Maniiḷaq, the regional nonprofit entity that managed tribal affairs in our region. (*Maniiḷaq* means "without money," and it also happens to be the name of a famous prophet who lived up the Kobuk River in the early 1800s.) Also with us were my lifelong friend Chuck Greene—Anaulaqtaq—who was mayor of the Northwest Arctic Borough, which we created when we invested in zinc mining. His brother, Frank "Ubie" Greene, was mayor of Kotzebue and manager of NANA's properties in town. Frank and Ubie's cousin Al Adams—Sikaaġruk—was our state senator. And I, at the time, was president of NANA.

Dennis's boat was made of aluminum. It must have been thirty feet long, and it had a huge jet engine that allowed it to zip along at an impressive clip despite the stupendous load of food, gear, and fuel we were carrying. We left Kotzebue and headed for Lockhart Point, past Pipe Spit, then over to one of the mouths of the Kobuk called Qitikliq. We finally decided to camp for the night on a slough off the main river. The boat was so big that there was room for all of us on board to stretch out on cots.

In the morning, we were having breakfast when a wooden boat pulled alongside. Its owner, a man named Badu, stopped for coffee, then moved on ahead of us in his smaller vessel.

We shoved off on the slough and revved up the big engine for the hundred-mile trip to our hunting site. As we rounded a long bend, we saw Badu's boat up ahead. He was poling his way along, which we thought was odd. We were tearing up the slough, figuring we were in the channel, almost to the main river. We were all bunched up next to the control panel near the bow, with Dennis driving and me standing behind all the others. We glanced at one another, grinning slightly because we thought we were so cool to be racing through the channel while Badu, up there, had to pole his boat.

All of a sudden, it was as if we had hit some monstrous invisible barrier. It was a sandbar. The water in this "channel" of ours was now only three inches deep, and we crashed to a stop within a matter of feet. The forty-gallon drum of fuel was not tied down, and it hurtled into us, with me, at the rear of the group, serving as the primary cushion for my companions.

It was like being hit by a Mack truck. For a moment I thought I had been crushed. I lay in the bow of the boat writhing in pain, wondering whether I would die. Anaulaqtaq leapt forward and held on to me as I squawked, "Arii, arii!" (It hurts!) The others managed to push the boat loose from the sandbar, and we headed for the village of Kiana, just a few miles up the river.

There I was barely able to make my way to the home of an assistant village health aide. Fortunately for me, she was at home, even though most of the villagers were away on hunting trips during the Labor Day holiday. She found some blood in my urine, and fearing that I might have suffered internal damage, put me on a plane to Kotzebue, where I checked into the hospital. I had two cracked ribs.

My friends continued the hunt. And I can say from experience that there's nothing worse than having to depend on your friends for your winter's meat supply. That adventure is still remembered by the people of the Kobuk River as another example of how little the *taġiuġmiut* ("saltwater people") know about the tricky freshwater channels and how quickly things can go wrong when out on the hunt.

Most hunting trips end more happily. I vividly remember one July, about twenty-five years ago, when a group of us went hunting for *ugruk*—bearded seal. We took a 24-foot Boston Whaler way out into Kotzebue Sound but couldn't get close enough to bag any seals. After lunch, I took the tiller. We navigated through the floes of old ice—heavy, thick formations built up over several long winters—that were floating through the Bering Sea toward the Arctic Ocean. I motored around one berg and there, just a hundred yards away, were four huge walrus basking in the sun.

Walrus are a protected species, but the Marine Mammal Protection Act allows the Iñupiat an exemption, permitting us to hunt walrus for subsistence purposes. We were ecstatic to see them, as they are not often found near Kotzebue. As quietly and slowly as possible, I maneuvered the boat toward the ice floe where the walrus were sunning themselves. Suddenly they spotted us and started scrambling for the sea. Just at that same instant two rifles blasted—and two of the walrus lay still. We had gotten enough meat and blubber for a winter, along with some much-coveted ivory, which Iñupiaq artists are permitted to use for an infinite variety of beautiful carvings.

And then there was the *usik*. *Usik* is a word an Iñupiaq normally would not speak aloud. But today, referring to walrus *usik* has become acceptable because the *naluaġmiut* use it all the time. The truth is that the male walrus is remarkably endowed. He has a permanent bone, eighteen to twenty-four inches long, that lines his reproductive organ and is safely ensconced near his tail. Once removed from the tough tissue that surrounds it, the bone is cleaned and dried and shined up, sometimes adorned with additional carvings, and serves as an extremely popular conversation piece. Don Young, Alaska's lone congressman, has been known to cow environmentalists by using a walrus *usik* as a gavel in committee meetings. I gave one to my friend Senator Daniel Inouye of Hawaii, who keeps it discreetly stashed in one of his Senate closets. A walrus *usik* even made an appearance once on Johnny Carson's *Tonight Show*. After sniffing and rubbing it, he almost dropped it when he learned that he was holding the male organ of a walrus!

One September in the late 1980s, my nephew George and I loaded up my Sportsman boat with gear and gasoline, intending to go after caribou. It was late in the month—cold, but not yet freezing—and the western Arctic herd would be making its way south for the winter from the treeless summer feeding grounds in the North Slope.

George and I had never hunted together before, but I was happy to have a strong teenager along in case we had some luck. We headed north to the mouth of the Little Noatak River about fifteen miles from Kotzebue and turned up toward Sigluaq ("food storage place"). Once there, we stopped and walked inland a way and climbed the hills to see if we could spot the herd.

From our new vantage point, we could see clear across the Noatak delta, with its myriad lakes and tributaries. Scanning the area, I noticed a dot in the distance on the far side of a large lake. I hadn't brought binoculars, but I thought that dot just might be a moose. Moose season was still open, so

George and I decided to go downriver and park the boat near where our family's old sod house had been. We would walk to the lake and *itchuq*—wait—to see if the moose might wander by.

Within an hour we were heading with our rifles up to a large stand of alders and willows near the lake, where I thought we might find a dry spot with a good vantage point. Unbeknownst to us, a huge moose, over seven feet tall with its giant antlers, was just feet away from us. As we nonchalantly walked into the brush, he suddenly charged out toward the lake, his legs flailing like crazy, acting as if he would run on the top of the water to escape these two completely startled hunters. I barely had time to get off a shot. By the time I did, he had made fair headway into the lake, and even after I fired, he kept going. I knew my shot was good, though. Sure enough, he was soon floating about twenty five yards out and not even quivering.

The problem was, he was like an iceberg. His head, horns, and a bit of belly were showing, but 90 percent of him was underwater. We had more than 500 pounds of lean, healthy, tasty, steroid-free meat out there—so near, and yet so far. How could we get it ashore?

The wind was cold and the water was colder, meaning that I couldn't swim out to the moose without risking hypothermia. Twenty years earlier, I would have been better equipped for such a situation: I would have had in my *nakmaġvik*—hunting bag—a wooden projectile with sharp barbs on a long, strong string we used to bring in ducks, geese, and muskrats that were too far out in the water to retrieve. I decided to improvise. I found a heavy metal fishhook, tied it to some nylon string, and attempted to cast it out to hook the moose. But the hook was too light and the wind too strong, and I could throw the hook only a few yards out. After trying that approach for an hour or so, George and I stopped to ponder our next move over coffee.

As it happened, just about then another relative, Billy, came up the river, saw my boat, and walked up to see how things were going. Billy had a pair of chest waders I thought might help me get closer to the moose. I put them on and started walking out into the water. But with each step I sank deeper into the muck, and I was not at all sure that I would be able to pull myself out if I got in too deep.

What now? I had already spent three hours trying to get that moose, and the notion of leaving game to rot is anathema to Iñupiat people. Finally I took my small hand ax to the river, where George and I found several small trees, trimmed them, and hauled them to the lake's edge. Using my nylon string, I constructed a raft that was just wide enough for me to mount. Wearing Billy's waders, I figured I could dangle my legs in the water and stay afloat if I could balance myself on the impromptu craft. I found a gaff hook in the boat, tied a small rope to it and curled it on my lap, and headed out toward the moose, using a spruce tree as an oar. George and Billy watched from the shore. I knew that if I fell in, probably the whole state would hear about it and I would never live it down. We love to tell stories that put our leaders in their place.

I paddled out to the moose. He had, for sure, expired, thank goodness. I swung the gaff hook and succeeded in penetrating the bottom of one ear. With that, my craft and I wobbled badly and almost tipped over, but I caught myself and slowly paddled backward. We had gotten our moose. But the real work was about to begin.

Butchering a moose in ice-cold water is not pleasant. Your

hands are freezing. You can't get a good grip on your knife because the moose's fat makes it so slick. And you have to cut through huge vertebrae and heavy chunks of meat. But we all pitched in to skin the moose and carve it into manageable pieces so that we could carry them to the boat, about two hundred yards away. We gave Billy a hindquarter and off he went to hunt some caribou.

By the time we carried the last load to the boat, it was about midnight. We were very tired but very happy as we headed slowly downriver in the darkness—occasionally missing the channel and running aground. But eventually we made it home. That winter we ate moose, and it was delicious.

Some years after the caribou hunt with my friends that came to such a bad end, Aġnaġaq and I decided to head up the river to see if we could have better luck with the caribou. Aġnaġaq—Fred—was the one who had delivered me from Nome when I was three. By this time he was in his late sixties, an inveterate smoker who had already lost one lung. We invited my nephew Johnny along, loaded my Boston Whaler with a drum of fuel, a small tent, and food and equipment, and off we headed toward the mouth of the Noatak River. I always felt comfortable when older family members were along on one of my hunts because I figured they knew where the deep water was. This time, though, it didn't take us long to hit shallow water and I lost a little faith in Fred, who was pointing the way.

Eventually we made it up the river into the hills and past the canyon to the western end of the Brooks Range. Our people call this Iġġich Isuat, "the end of the mountains." (The *naluaġmiut* call it the Baird Mountains, continuing a tradition that has always annoyed me: Outsiders were always pinning names on our territory that bore no relation to the people who have occupied the area for thousands of years and who for untold generations have known every key geographic feature in intimate detail.)

Two or three other boats were already at Iġġich Isuat when we arrived, so we stopped for coffee with the other hunters, all of whom we knew. Among them were Herman Barger and some of his sons. Herman was a little younger than Fred and had lived near my sister Annie on the beach in Kotzebue most of his life.

After coffee, we saw a sizable herd of about fifty caribou quite a distance away up the small tributary that emptied into the Noatak. Most of the others didn't want to make the difficult trek across the hills and tussocks, but Herman and I and one of his sons decided to go take a look. We headed up the hill.

The herd was moving away from us, and we had to walk much farther than we originally thought to keep up. By the time we got close enough to fire, we must have been three miles from the camp. We blasted away. One caribou fell. The problem was, we didn't have any packboards to help cart out the animal. We butchered it into five main pieces—the hind end, two front quarters, and two sets of ribs. Herman grabbed the hind end, which was pretty heavy, and sat it on his shoulders, holding on to the legs. I picked up the rib cage with the vertebrae attached and carried it like a log across my own shoulders. Herman and his son took the front and hindquarters. Then we headed back to camp, feeling pretty good about all the meat.

It was getting late in the day and cooling off pretty fast, but we were sweating hard as we made our way across the tundra, stepping between the tussocks. It was incredibly taxing work, and our load was unbearably heavy. I thought my neck bones were being crushed. We'd walk several hundred yards, then stop, flinging down the meat for a rest. Finally we made it back to camp, and were met with a surprise.

While we had gone halfway to hell and back, the rest of the caribou had walked right into the camp. Not a dozen yards from our own boat, with a bare minimum of effort and toil, Aġnaġaq and Johnny had killed four of them!

That night, winter decided to set in. The temperature dropped like a stone and the river began to freeze under the starlit sky. We were in good shape, since we had put up our tent and were well equipped with a primus stove, sleeping bags, and candles. One of the other boats wasn't so well prepared, and to keep warm through the night, they had to build a bonfire.

When I awoke, it was still dark. Aġnaġaq was already awake, and I could see the bright red of his cigarette as he drew on it with his one lung. I stirred and said, "*Allapaa*" (It's cold). I put on my parka and lit the stove, putting the water on for coffee just as I used to do when I was a kid. It didn't take too long for the air to warm inside the tent. The coffee boiled and the aroma permeated the entire tent, just as I remembered from forty years earlier.

I was not sure how we were going to break our way through the ice on the river in order to make our way home. But the sun came out and warmed the air and a wind arose and began to break up the ice. We packed the boat with our load of caribou, a half tank of fuel, our equipment and food, and Johnny, Aġnaġaq, and I headed downriver.

The wind was cold and strong, gusting at 20 or 30 miles an hour. Whitecaps formed in the river and raged straight at us. I had never seen anything like it—most rivers in the area are relatively calm. But we took our time and made it down to the mouth of the Noatak, then headed into the lagoon behind Kotzebue with our generous load of meat.

Sadly, Aġnaġaq died just a couple of years after that memorable trip. He had lived through a lot, and he had survived to become an elder. But one night, when he was drinking, he fell and froze to death. And Herman Barger, who at the age of sixty-five was tough enough to carry the hind end of a good-size caribou three miles across the tundra, also died not long after our hunt.

Two good men from the old generation left the rest of us to continue trying to find our way. We had traveled together to Iġġich Isuat, the end of the mountains, and they had come to *tumi isua*, the end of their trail.

22

Iñuit Katırut: The Iñuit Gather

Eben Hopson and I had a lot in common, despite the fact that he was nearly twenty years older than me. He was born of a part *naluaġmiut* father and an Iñupiaq mother. He'd never had the opportunity to go to high school or college; his formal education went no further than the Barrow Day School, one of the institutions run by the Bureau of Indian Affairs. But he was very smart, and went on to become a force to be reckoned with in territorial, state, and local politics.

In 1970, when I was elected to the state Senate, Eben became a special assistant to Bill Egan, who was reelected governor that year. Together we worked on a number of projects, including the final approval of the land settlement. We also pushed hard to ensure the creation of the North Slope Borough, the vast municipal district that encompassed most of the oil-related commerce stemming from the development of Prudhoe Bay. Four years later, when I resigned as president of the Alaska Federation of Natives in order to make my unsuccessful run for the U.S. Congress, I paved the way for Eben to succeed me at the AFN. We were united in our determination to improve the lives of village people by pushing for local control and developing institutions our own people could run.

By 1977, Eben was mayor of the North Slope Borough he had helped to establish, confronting the hard task of modernizing villages that still lacked the rudiments of a decent life—schools, power plants, clinics, housing, roads, and water and sewer facilities. After years of legal wrangling with Big Oil, whose executives were apoplectic at the idea of Iñupiat control over anything to do with petroleum resources, Eben had made a difficult peace with the industry. Revenues from oil development were flowing into the coffers of the North Slope Borough, and he had the means to try to reverse generations of want and struggle among his people. But making progress was not easy. Eben faced entrenched opposition in his community. As I had come to understand when I was in the state legislature, representing Barrow as well as Kotzebue, Eben had to contend with a number of warring factions, based both on long-standing local animosities and on fierce rivalry over the considerable financial and political power involved in dispensing jobs and contracts. Barrow is the North Slope Borough seat, a clan town due to competition that arose during the whaling days, with different clan leaders jockeying for political leadership and respect. These divisions still play out in the local politics.

Eben had not traveled much beyond Alaska. But he was fully aware that Iñuit culture was scattered clear across Earth's icy crown and that it was considerably older than the four modern nations—the Soviet Union, Canada, the United States, and Denmark—that had divided up the traditional Iñuit homelands. He was also aware that Alaska was not the only place where significant change was affecting the Iñuit in the last quarter of the twentieth century. In Greenland, for example, our brethren were working out the terms of home rule with the Danish government. For the first time in the modern era, that predominantly Iñuit territory was to be ruled by its own people.

There were also international issues in play that affected all Iñuit people. In the United States, for instance, there was growing sentiment in favor of outlawing whaling, and Eben heard that President Jimmy Carter was leaning toward supporting such a prohibition. Meanwhile, Canada had started permitting offshore oil exploration, a move that alarmed Iñupiat whalers because of the danger of spills and blowouts. So when John Buchholdt, Eben's confidant and adviser, suggested an international conference of whalers to discuss the issues confronting them, Eben jumped at the idea—and expanded on it. Before long, the whaling convention had morphed into the first-ever meeting of the Iñuit from around the globe (although this first meeting did not include Iñuit from the Soviet Union; they would come later). The goal became to form an organization, an enduring one, that would fight jointly on behalf of the world's 150,000 Iñuit in matters both political and cultural.

From the very first, the gathering carried a special excitement. It had been five thousand years since the Iñuit had been together. Now, here in Barrow, the yellowish red midnight sun shimmered among the ice floes. There were perhaps a thousand of us. We celebrated the fact that we continued to exist despite being splintered among four countries. We recounted to one another how in each of the nations of our diaspora we had tried to find our way, fighting to keep from being submerged and disappearing among our own countrymen. We compared languages, danced, drank, hugged, prayed, sang. All of us loved to sing hymns. And we found that the Greenlanders, in particular, excelled at musical harmony—the women dressed in elaborately beaded shawls, sealskin shorts, and thigh-high sealskin mukluks with intricate designs, and the men in snow-white anoraks, black slacks, and black mukluks. We celebrated as long as our bodies didn't fail us and slept only long enough to resume the orgy of Iñupiaq communication that had so long eluded us.

The formal business of the conference was more difficult. When I got to Barrow, I realized that there had not been much planning. Once the opening speeches were over, there was no blueprint for what would follow. Eben, long accustomed to wearing down opponents and getting his way, had drafted some articles and bylaws for the new organization. But it was soon clear that our guests were not about to be manhandled into approving a structure and processes they'd had no hand in creating.

As it turned out, I became something of a prime minister for Eben. I knew that what was really important to him was to be recognized as the founder and head of the new organization. I accepted that as goal number one. Goal number two, it seemed to me, was to come up with a design for the organization that the Iñuit from Canada and Greenland would find acceptable.

We weren't properly set up for instant translations, and for a while our wonderful euphoria was in danger of being lost in translation, so to speak. But I remembered how we had dealt with the initial gathering of the Alaska Federation of Natives back in 1966. We created committees in which delegates could work to figure out a way forward. I suggested to Eben that we set up a similar process for this organization—a committee structure that would do the detail work and then present proposals at the next general assembly.

That is just what we ended up doing. A Resolutions Committee, made up of me, Robert Petersen of Greenland, and Bill Edmunds of Quebec, was set up to review all resolutions and put them in proper form for voting. Ultimately we decided that each of the three countries represented at the conference would appoint four people to a committee that would be charged with proposing a constitution and bylaws to the next general assembly, which was to be held three years later in Nuuk, Greenland, in 1980.

We declared the Iñuit Circumpolar Council in existence and named Eben Hopson its president. The conference erupted in cheers, ovations, and hugs, the initial euphoria enveloping us once again. Then we disbanded to the four corners of the Iñuit world.

While we were coming together, we were also beginning to come apart. A schism was developing among the Iñupiat. After a thousand years of contact with the Europeans, the Greenlanders had developed left, right, and center politicians. In Alaska, we were so new to the game of politics that we barely knew those terms. But divisions along those very lines—particularly on the North Slope—were becoming impossible to ignore. Internal politics was pitting generation against generation, young against old, and there was clan politics as well. Eben represented the older generation. Before the Iñuit gathering, he had made peace, or so he thought, with two representatives of the young Turks, Billy Neakok and Charlie Etok Edwardsen. Although they were more radical than Eben, and distrusted the oil companies and consultants who were so important in the North Slope, Eben even hired them as employees of the North Slope Borough.

The four Alaskan representatives named to the constitution and bylaws committee of the Inuit Circumpolar Council were Eben Hopson, Billy Neakok, Etok Edwardsen, and me. The Canadians named Charlie Watt, Bill Edmunds, Bill Gordon, and Mary Sillett; Robert Petersen, Hans-Pavia Rosing, Angmalortoq Olsen, and Ove Rosing Olsen were the members from Greenland.

Unfortunately, after two meetings of the committee, the Alaskan contingent blew apart. Billy Neakok declared he would run against Eben Hopson for mayor of the North Slope Borough, so Eben summarily fired both him and Etok. For a while, the future of our ambitious vision was in serious doubt. Then Eben had an idea. We would resurrect the Resolutions Committee, which I had chaired during the conference. That committee—far more manageable than the unwieldy constitution and bylaws group—would continue the work of designing a structure for the Iñuit Circumpolar Council.

For the next three years, Eben and I were pilloried across the Arctic by the left wing of the Iñuit world, a faction we came to call "the Red Guard." They accused us of violating the directions of the general assembly by working on the constitution and bylaws after our Alaskan contingent had fallen apart, and charged that the work we were doing to design a new constitution would be illegal because we were doing it under the aegis of the resurrected Resolutions Committee. In the meantime, Eben fell ill with cancer, and died at the age of fifty-eight. I had met with him in the hospital when he still had energy and he made it clear that he wanted me to continue the efforts he had begun to create the inner workings of the ICC. I had no choice. It was an obligation I had to carry out.

When it came time for the second general assembly of the Iñuit Circumpolar Council, we put together a charter flight that would take Alaska's and Canada's delegations to Greenland. By that time, after all the accusations about our work being illegal, I was somewhat dispirited. I felt that the Arctic Slope leaders who had taken over after Eben's death—many of whom were more interested in the corporate side of things, and less in the legislative side Eben worked so hard to develop—were not supporting the ICC wholeheartedly. I could not bear to face all the negativity over something Eben had believed in so fervently, and at the last minute I did not board the jet that carried our delegation to Greenland.

But my conscience got the better of me. I climbed on a commercial flight to Copenhagen, then flew on to Greenland. I arrived in Nuuk just in time to see the gregarious Iñuit spirit about to founder. Delegates unaware of the difficult politics of the past three years were making motions that were going nowhere, and there was the usual confusion about translating all the motions on the table. The revered Robert Petersen of Greenland was at the chair. Dr. Petersen, a teacher and historian, was considered a wise man, one of Greenland's most respected public figures. Soft-spoken and well-educated, he was not accustomed to the rough-and-tumble of politics, and was having great trouble keeping the meeting in order. There was no one present who might have figured out what the ever-resourceful Eben Hopson would have done to keep things under control.

Furthermore, trouble was on the way in the person of

Etok Edwardsen, one of the ringleaders of the Red Guard. Etok was not a delegate to the conference and so had not been permitted to ride on the charter jet, but it was rumored he was nevertheless heading to Greenland with like-minded friends, who were planning to challenge the constitution and bylaws the Resolutions Committee had designed—not that they had any alternatives to offer. Several of us gathered to figure out what to do. In the middle of this discussion, my sense of proportion reasserted itself. It suddenly occurred to me: if the Iñuit of the world—tiny in numbers and long accustomed to living in close quarters despite their differences—could not work out our problems, we simply didn't deserve to have an organization.

We let the Red Guard members land. When Etok showed up at the conference and tried to take the floor to speak, I gaveled him out of order as a nondelegate and continued the meeting. Etok then asked Charlie Watt, an Iñuk leader from Quebec and the head of the Makivik Corporation, to speak for him. Before Watt began, I gaveled the delegates to attention and asked for an executive session.

Behind the scenes, I proceeded to explain to the Iñuit leaders what had transpired since our first meeting. I told them how the Alaskan contingent of the constitution and bylaws committee had self-destructed and how the Resolutions Committee, which after all did have the imprimatur of the general assembly, had stepped in to do the work. If there were questions about the legality of this process, or problems with the constitution and bylaws we had designed, I said, the remedy was simple: the full committee established in the first general assembly could review our work in a separate meeting and present its findings to the general assembly.

That is exactly what happened. The full committee reviewed the work—and did not change a single phrase. The work of the Resolutions Committee was adopted by the general assembly.

With that, we had the real organization Eben Hopson had envisioned—one that would strengthen unity among us, stand up for our rights on the international stage, and promote the development of Iñuit culture. Even the Red Guard had to be grudgingly satisfied, as the vote was nearly unanimous. Everyone stood, clasped hands, and cheered.

23

Puttuqsriruŋa: Epiphany in Nome

For ten thousand years, the desolate beach along Norton Sound on the southern shore of the Seward Peninsula was part of the territory where the Iñupiat fished and hunted and camped, building homes of sod on the treeless coastline. But it was never an Iñupiat community like Kotzebue. And when, in the late nineteenth century, gold was discovered on these beaches, whatever chance it might have had to develop a sense of community was shattered. The area was flooded by *naluaġmiut* eager to make their fortunes. There were 30,000 of them, and they came from all over the world. Inevitably, our people, too, were drawn to the place, where the burgeoning mining and related commerce made it possible to trade for necessary items and earn badly needed cash. It was a rare Iñuk indeed who could resist the Wild West trappings of the place, where white traders were glad to sell them alcohol and anything else they could foist upon them. The city that sprouted from the gold craze—Nome—always had a colonial frontier mentality, and from its earliest days it was the focal point of efforts to convert our people and control their lives through laws and regulations.

As a candidate for state office, I always got a headache when I went to Nome. I never really knew why until I found myself there in the winter of 1980, walking along the beach, alone. By then the gold was mostly gone and the town had shrunk to 3,000 souls. A breakwater of huge rocks protected the beaches from the winter storms. There were bars galore, at least ten churches, and, on the south end of town, a whole village of King Islanders, who had moved from their island when the Bureau of Indian Affairs shut down their school. Walking along the beach, I thought that, for all I knew, this might have been just yards from the site of the shack where I *qauġri*—became aware of my surroundings—and that was not a pretty scene. It had been thirty-five years since Fred Hensley—Aġnaġaq—rescued me and my sister from that miserable life and brought us home to Kotzebue.

Like many of my colleagues, I reflected, I was part of the flotsam and jetsam of our little world. Rejected by my mother, unrecognized by my father, adopted and reared by my great-uncle, raised by my loving adopted mother in the twilight of her years, I received a formal education that found nothing of value in our Iñupiaq culture, and I struggled to find myself in the turmoil of the sixties.

I remember visiting a college friend from George Washington University in his upscale neighborhood in a Philadelphia suburb, in 1964. It was on that same day that a massive earthquake registering 8.4 on the Richter scale decimated large parts of Alaska. My classmate's father made a comment I have never forgotten: that I would be better off downplaying the fact that I was an Iñupiaq and an Alaskan. I have no idea what inspired him to say that, but it brought back various remarks I had heard from non-Native Alaskans about the dirty, shiftless, lazy Natives who would be better off abandoning their backward, savage ways. If they didn't say it out loud, their actions and laws made it clear they saw very little of value in our culture.

On that wintry beach in Nome, I had an epiphany. For the first time, I suddenly recognized the full extent of the human suffering that had been taking place among our people in the least obvious of places: in our minds and spirits. For the first time, I truly began to understand some profound truths about the nature of identity, culture, and connection and about the systematic measures—especially religious and educational indoctrination—used by nations all over the world to destroy the spirit of the minorities within their borders.

I had been going nonstop for fifteen years, since the day the realization hit me like a thunderbolt that our people were on the verge of losing our homeland. I had driven myself to exhaustion trying to improve the lives of our people through the state legislature, through the Northwest Alaska Native Association, the Alaska Federation of Natives, the Alaska Village Electric Cooperative, and the Land Claims Task Force. In the meantime, I had married, divorced, remarried, and had four children.

My cohorts and I had all been extending ourselves tremendously, both physically and mentally, doing what we felt we had to do to uplift ourselves, our families, and our people. We were not politicians; we became politicians. We were not businessmen; we became businessmen. We were not managers; we became managers. The pressures had been enormous. For fifteen years, we had focused almost exclusively on trying to win back our land, setting up our regional corporations to implement the land settlement, and doing everything we could to elevate our people from their dire economic circumstances. We built warmer homes, we installed electricity and safe water systems, we improved sanitary conditions. We pushed for clinics and village schools and for projects that could bring incomes to local workers. In short, we had been trying to accomplish in a single generation the monumental task of uplifting an entire people from poverty and involving them in the making of laws and policies that affected all aspects of their lives.

But now I had come to a dead end. It was not a crossroads. I realized with a dreadful clarity that all the political and economic activity of the past fifteen years had not really brought better lives for our people. Sure, we were not starving or freezing the way we used to and our health care facilities were improving. But there was a yawning pit out there, and in spite of our best efforts, we were sliding downhill, straight into it. We were becoming alcoholic or violent, committing suicide, neglecting children, beating wives, and going to jail in greater numbers than ever before.

My own family was a microcosm of the larger problem. Naungaġiaq and Aqpayuk's son Isaac—Auleniq—froze to death from exposure in Anchorage, where he had gone for alcohol treatment. Aġnaġaq, who had rescued Saigulik and me from Nome, froze to death after hitting his head during a drinking spell. My birth mother, Makpiiq, died an alcoholic. My cousin Elizabeth was also an alcoholic and lost two husbands to the disease, although she herself died of cancer. Bull Hensley, a nephew, drowned in his own vomit. So did Benny's wife, Irene Hensley, who left behind eight children. One of my nephews tried to kill himself with a rifle while in an alcoholic daze, but fortunately survived the attempt. Even as a boy, I was aware that whenever Naungaġiaq heard her boys were drinking, she would stay away from home. And in the end, she died in a church, homeless because one of her

sons had sold the family house to bail himself out of jail for
public drunkenness.

There was something drastically wrong and no one had
put a finger on the cause. In my own life, I had been a failure as a husband and father, putting all my energies into
building up NANA's business portfolio—establishing our
solid-waste and sewage treatment utility at Prudhoe Bay,
organizing United Bank Alaska and Alaska United Drilling.
My young children might have thought they were fatherless
in those years, as I desperately tried to fit them into my frantic schedule. I was too preoccupied to be much of a husband.
But that night in Nome, I finally began to understand the nature of my own situation as well as our collective experience.

All of us were part of the continuum of our people going
back tens of thousands of years, from the glacial epoch to the
present. Yet in less than two hundred years, our world had
gone through a maelstrom of change. It had begun when the
first Russians noticed the existence of what the Aleuts called
Alyeska and began the massive effort to secure the riches its
land and waters contained—killing and enslaving the Aleuts
to hunt for them. It accelerated after the Treaty of Cession in
1867, as the United States sought to prove that Secretary of
State William H. Seward's "folly"—paying Russia $7.2 mil-
lion for control of Alaska—was actually an extraordinarily
wise investment. The onslaught against the sea otters,
whales, seals, walrus, fish, and fur-bearing animals sped up
furiously, as did the deliberate destruction of Native cultures,
Iñupiat, Yupik, Aleut, Athapascan, Tlingit, and Haida. The
discovery of gold in the Klondike and on the beaches of
Nome only made matters worse, changing forever the face of
northwest Alaska. People poured in from all corners of the
earth. The animal life upon which the Native people depended came under more and more pressure. Native popula-

tions were decimated by *naluaġmiut*-introduced disease, epidemics of influenza, diphtheria, chicken pox, measles, and tuberculosis.

The cultural war against us was even more deadly. Generation after generation, our people were told that they were not adequate, did not measure up, and had to change from who they were into someone else. Our old religion was repressed. Our languages were virtually banned. Our dances were denounced as pagan and sinful. Our names were summarily changed.

When I was growing up, of course, I didn't see these things. My ignorance was doubtless exacerbated by feelings of inferiority. I was fatherless, an *aapaiḷauraq*, I was of mixed blood, our family was poor, I was always dirty, and I never had warm clothes. I could sense the condescension of *naluaġmiut* toward "the Natives," and could not help but notice the whiff of superiority they exuded in running the courts, the welfare system, the schools, and commerce.

But in Nome, at the age of forty, I finally began to understand the nature of the disconnections that had been taking place within our families and within our communities. I saw, for the first time, how well-meaning missionaries, intent on saving the souls of our people, joined in an unholy alliance with the federal government to remake Alaska Natives in their image. Their main tools were the church and the classroom. Hour by hour, day after day, year upon year, the educational system that had so efficiently assimilated millions of immigrants and hundreds of thousands of American Indians in the Lower Forty-eight worked its way into the nooks and crannies of Native Alaskan minds, crowding out the knowledge of a people who had spent ten thousand years learning through experience and observation about the beloved land that had nurtured us.

Starting at the turn of the last century, the *naluaġmiut* had the children from September to June of every year, a system put in place by Sheldon Jackson, the Presbyterian mission organizer who was appointed to run Alaska's educational system. Jackson, described by one historian as "the Napoleon of the United States government in all matters cultural and educational in Alaska,"* believed, as he wrote:

> If the Natives of Alaska could be taught the English language, be brought under Christian influences by the missionaries and trained into forms of industry suitable for the territory, it seems to follow as a necessary result that the white population of Alaska, composed of immigrants from the States, would be able to employ them in their pursuits, using their labor to assist in mining, transportation, and the production of food. (from the *Report of the Commissioner of Education for the Year 1896–1897* [Washington, D.C.: Government Printing Office, 1898], vol. I, p. xliv)

Nowhere in the system Jackson built up between 1889 and 1907 was there any mechanism that allowed the Native people any say whatsoever in the most basic of human endeavors. The bearded little "Napoleon" was interested only in creating a workforce for the emerging white majority.

As late as the 1960s, when I was a ticket agent for Wien Airlines, my first day on the job was writing tickets for hundreds of youngsters traveling from their villages through Kotzebue in a mass annual migration to Indian schools far from home. These schools were designed not to reinforce

*Glenn Smith, "Education for the Natives of Alaska: The Work of the United States Bureau of Education, 1884–1931," *Journal of the West*, vol. VI, no. 3 (July 1967): 441.

their identity, but to destroy it. In the place of a well-rounded individual who knew who he was, who knew his language, his family's history, and the values that sustained his people, the powers that be wanted an individual trained in arithmetic, English, American history, and economics—an individual who might become a mechanic, a secretary, a carpenter, or an upholsterer.

My family let me go just as others let their children go. They had faith that the new way would help them to a better life. They couldn't know the truth—that in reality, we were being set adrift, forced to find our way the best we could. Without parents to guide us, we were buffeted by all the conflicts of cultural change, facing teenage problems with no one to confide in, encountering temptations with no one to advise us, and trying to get by without any financial support. Nowhere in the academic landscape did we encounter even a suggestion that there was anything of value in our previous life. The teachers were completely ignorant of the rich cultures the children came from. It is no wonder that, in time, we began to question the value and worth of ourselves and of our people.

In 1995 and 1996, high school students from the Northwest Arctic Borough school district gathered oral histories for a publication called *Noorvik Elders*. In the stories told by the elders, you can plainly hear how hard the teachers worked to make them into good little English-speaking paradigms.

Mildred Iġluġuq Sampson was eighty-two years old when she spoke with the students. She had been born in Deering, a gold-mining town east of Kotzebue, but a Quaker missionary had persuaded many of the villagers to move across the sound to Noorvik, away from the raucous mining environment. "When I go to school, no noise at school, just quiet because our teachers use to tell us to study and they always say be quiet. When a person disobey, he would get punished and have to write one hundred sentences. Sometimes teachers get mad easy and slap them with a hammer on the hand." The schools had required students to speak English from 9:00 a.m. until 6:00 p.m. each day; Iġluġuq said, "I wish they didn't do that. The children would know how to speak Eskimo. They don't understand me so I have to speak English."

Other elders told the students of the punishments they suffered when they tried to use their own language—and how school authorities encouraged students to tell on each other. Helen Tullugalik Wells, born to a family of eleven children in 1926, said she made it only to sixth grade, and didn't attend school often, since she had to help her mother with younger siblings. But she remembered clearly, "They try not to let us talk Eskimo. You miss [the] party when you talk Eskimo. Other students watch you, too. If you talk Eskimo, they tell [the] teacher. No party." Similarly, Hazel Qitiqliilaq Snyder, whose parents had eighteen children, said she could attend school only about two and a half months a year. "When I talk Eskimo in school," she said, "they always pick me up and say, 'Pungalik talk Eskimo.' I had to write so many hundred 'I must speak English all the time.' "

Our elderly recognized the importance of learning the language of the church and government, and their patient comments—containing no public criticism of the rigid and autocratic practices of their teachers—is characteristic of our people. But it is absolutely apparent to me that this punitive denigration of our language and culture had a negative effect on our self-perception that has continued for generations.

As the system drummed our languages out of us, it became more and more difficult to communicate—impossible to have a meaningful conversation with parents and grandparents when you returned home. I can only imagine the sorrow our elders must have felt when they were no longer able to convey their feelings and knowledge to children and grandchildren who had been disconnected from them both physically and spiritually. The fruits of a better life, it seems, could be bitter.

So for all these years, generation after generation, we had been fighting to maintain some sense of equilibrium even as communication between generations slipped and ceased, and ancient notions of civility and duty faded. In the face of prejudice and discrimination, some of our people began to deny their Native identity. In a sense, it was not just our language and culture and knowledge that were fading away, it was our spirit—the very spirit that had allowed us to thrive and survive and overcome the elements for so long, the spirit that allowed us to cross oceans in our *umiaq* and *qayaq*, the spirit that enabled our people to rejoice in the simplest of nature's creations and to create songs and dances of community and joy.

The revelation that came to me in Fairbanks in 1966—that our land was in jeopardy and we had to act immediately to save it—had led to a desperate scramble for a solution, and we had succeeded in finding it. This revelation was different. As I considered the inner world of spirit, identity, self-respect, and continuity that we seemed to be losing forever, I could see only a dead end. It seemed to me to be something akin to Dante's *Inferno*—a terrible, heartbreaking vision of oppression, prejudice, and the destruction of a people through every means imaginable. After that, what could be the way forward?

This is where I was at that point in my life. It is as clear to me now as it was then. I could not hold back the tears of sorrow. They simply engulfed me as I considered, that night in Nome, the generations of our people who had experienced this catastrophe. I wept for myself, for my family, for my friends, for my people, for our ancestors. I cried for those who had drunk themselves into oblivion or simply turned off their Native consciousness, for those who could cope no longer and had ended their lives.

I felt useless, as if all the things I had fought for had been for naught. I was without hope. And as I often had before, when circumstances became too much for me, I headed for home, for Kotzebue. That was where my spirit was most comfortable.

24

Qianak! Sivutmun!: Don't Cry! Move Forward!

A good friend delivered me to the airport in Nome to catch
the short flight to Kotzebue. She had seen a grown Iñupiaq
man break down and sob, and I'm certain that she had no
idea what had happened to me in Nome, what had caused
such a powerful reaction.

Shouldn't I have been walking on clouds? We had concluded the creation of the Iñuit Circumpolar Council, uniting
the Iñuit of the polar world, in the northernmost community
in the United States. We had moved the entire U.S. Congress
to pass the most sweeping and fairest Native American land
settlement; we had changed the corporate landscape of
Alaska with the creation of twelve regional corporations run
by Alaska Natives with a land base of 44 million acres; we
had almost $1 billion to invest; the North Slope Iñuit had
created America's largest municipality that could tax the oil
companies at Prudhoe Bay; and we had organized the Alaska
Federation of Natives—the first organization in ten thousand

years that united all Alaska Natives. Yet here I was, almost prostrate in despair. Had I misplaced my priorities? Had I misled our people?

When the plane landed in Kotzebue, I was whisked off on a snow machine by my nephew Johnny Qipqiñia Schaeffer— "the General," as I call him. We were headed for Ivik, about thirty miles north of Kotzebue, where my sister Annie lived and where Johnny and several other nephews and nieces have cabins.

About halfway there, we stopped at Ikkattuq, the scene of so many of my fond early memories. Now the place where my family had lived off the land was a cemetery for my brothers Umiivik, Auleniq, and Saqik. The old sod house had collapsed, and was slowly, inevitably, returning to nature. Johnny and I spent some time reflecting on how much we enjoyed life out in the tundra and recalling the youth and vigor that had once permeated these premises. Then we roared off to Ivik.

Ivik means grass, and not surprisingly, the ground there beyond the gravel beach on the protected little bay is high and grassy. Beyond the clutch of cabins, spruce trees line the foothills and the land rises gently to Indian Mountain, a promontory several hundred feet high that affords a 360-degree view of the surrounding land and waters. It is easy walking, as the mountain is bald. It is a wonderful place to look for caribou, and has been used as a lookout since the dawn of our time.

There was never any to-do when I arrived to see Annie (Iġluġuq) and her husband, John (Aġutuq). They loved the country, and I am not sure they were really even aware of the pressure and stress of the political side of my life—a world that was quite foreign to them. Annie and I had become acquainted when I was twelve years old. It was a great joy to learn that she was my sister, and gave me a window onto a part of my life—my father's side—that I was only vaguely aware of. She had been raised in an orphanage by Catholic nuns and in boarding schools run by the Bureau of Indian Affairs. She was a beauty in her youth, tiny and tough.

I was always intimidated by my brother-in-law, a handsome man, half Iñupiaq and half German, and the epitome of the strong, capable, stoic hunter. John had lost his own father early and became a breadwinner for his mother and sisters, fishing and hunting in traditional style and taking any paying work he could find. Annie and John had a large family—ten living children by the time of my visit. Both of them wanted their children to thrive in the new economy. I once asked Annie once why she didn't teach her children Iñupiaq and she replied, "So they wouldn't have to suffer like we did."

But Annie and John provided just the loving and pleasant atmosphere—and the comforting *niqipiaq*, native food—I needed to help bring me back down to earth. I was prepared to stay as long as it took to restore my troubled psyche and resolve my dilemma. I had reached the point where I was not sure that all the energy I had put into politics and business was doing any good. If not, what should I be doing from that point on?

For the next week I stayed put at Ivik. I chopped wood and walked, all the while trying to unscramble the confusion in my mind. Mostly I faced the central question: Was there any way forward, considering the damage that had been done to our people's identity and self-worth, our language, our values, and our knowledge of our culture? It seemed to me that we all had been cast adrift. Now, as individuals, each of us could only hope to find some life raft or anchor that would keep us safe and sane in a world that no longer made communal sense to us.

As I pondered our history, my initial reaction was rage. There were so many villains in the piece that it was almost impossible to settle on who was most to blame. The government had taken our children away and turned them against our language and culture. The missionaries had damned our dances and silenced our songs and denounced our spirit world as unworthy. The greedy traders had gypped our people and happily siphoned off their hard-won earnings as payment for swamping us with tobacco and alcohol.

Silently, furiously, during those days at Ivik I tallied up the list of those who had damaged us so deeply. There were the GIs who made our men feel impotent as they chased our women, and the judges who wielded life-defining power over people who had no knowledge of the language of the court. There were the faceless politicians in Washington who made fish and game rules we had to break in order to feed our families, and the Alaskan politicians who had barred our elderly from the Pioneer Homes and who had permitted the despicable signs: NO DOGS OR NATIVES ALLOWED.

There seemed to be no end to the oppressors who had taken advantage of us as we tried, every way we knew how, to be good citizens. But finally I settled on what in my mind was the most destructive force of all: the Bureau of Indian Affairs and its repressive school system, which had served as the main weapon against our language, our culture, and our children's spirits.

Of course, I could not ignore the part our own people had played in this drama. For so many years, for so many lifetimes, our parents and grandparents had been compliant participants in the demolishing of our languages, our values, our history, and, in the end, our self-respect and our identity. They had believed what the government and the missionaries told them: that their children would be better off if they let them go. They couldn't see that in setting the children adrift, they were sowing the seeds of their people's cultural demise.

And we younger generations were also at fault. What on earth had happened to the idea that had energized me and others when we began to fight for our traditional lands? We wanted them so that our people could exist as they always had, drawing on the riches of the land and sea and air. We wanted the land so that we could continue to live as Iñupiaq people, so that we could run our own affairs and, in time, find our own way to accommodate modernization.

Now here we were, running about in a frenzy, planning and accounting and investing and managing and traveling. Without realizing it, I and my Iñupiaqati had allowed our spirit and culture to take a backseat to pressing corporate and political issues. In so doing, we were crowding out the very thing we had fought for in the first place: the consciousness of our people's heritage, purpose, and survival as a culture. It seemed to me that we had lost our way, charging into the future without any idea of what we were really doing and why. We were digging our own cultural grave.

I suppose, if I had any self-destructive tendencies, this would have been a good time to go. However, deep inside, I knew that the Iñupiaq were not a people who gave up in the face of struggle. Our people had made a life on the farthest fringe of the polar world. We had fought cold and deprivation, and through the ingenuity of the mind we had created implements and art from stone, flint, jade, ivory, bone, and wood and every usable part of the living world that helped us to survive. We had even turned snow into shelter and sod into a palace of warmth. Through trial and error, we had mastered the environment and passed on that knowledge through five hundred generations.

During that week in Ivik, I had a strong sense of why we were the way we were. But where were our philosophers? Where were our politicians? Where were the standard-bearers who would speak the words that needed to be said? *Quit killing us. There is value and worth in our people.*

As Johnny and I sped back toward Kotzebue on the snow machine, these questions completely dominated my thoughts. I did not know the answers. But I knew that finding them was essential. And then, somewhere between Ivik and Kotzebue—it might even have been at Ikkattuq, as we sped by—I realized that laying blame would never resolve the dilemma we faced. It would simply serve to avoid the issue. While it would be useful to show our people where we had been and what had happened to us, we had to put that behind us and confront the issues that lay ahead. In true Iñupiaq fashion, we had to move forward, to put to work the good spirit that is innate in our people.

25

Iñupiat Iḷitqusiat: The Iñupiat Spirit

The people had permitted me to be a leader for fifteen years, and a leader has the obligation of providing hope, even when the situation appears hopeless. So when I got back to Kotzebue, I called a meeting of all the key figures in the community—from the tribe, the elders, the corporations, the school district, and other institutions—everyone who had a concern for the well-being of our people. I had no unique status. I was not an elder. I was not *the* leader, just *a* leader. I was just someone who cared. And, I was to discover, I was not alone.

The community leaders responded just as they had in 1966, when our land was threatened. We assembled, about seventy-five strong, at Kotzebue's Senior Center. I had no plan and no agenda, no idea what I would say. I just knew that from a cultural perspective, there appeared to be no hope for our survival unless we began preserving our identity and the special qualities that were the essence of our people. Up to that point, as far as I knew, no one had ever articulated—for our children or for the outside world—the unique qualities of the Iñupiaq way. Always, the message to us had been that our way of life was doomed, that our language was passé, that our names must be changed, that our dances were sinful, that our homes stank, that *we* stank, and that the *aŋatkut*, our medicine men or shamans, were evil and had no positive aspects. We had never answered back, never explained to those who did not understand why our way was valuable and good—worthy of preservation. We had never enumerated the great strengths of a culture whose children were reared to know right from wrong, whose members went out of their way to assist people in need, who respected each other and the property of their neighbors, who were able to live together generation after generation without any semblance of heavy-handed government and with no such thing as a police force.

There, in the Senior Center, I stood before friends, relatives, coworkers, and a smattering of *naluaġmiut*, groping for how to begin. Suddenly a guiding spirit showed me the way. I began describing my epiphany in Nome.

"If we don't want to survive as Iñupiaq people, the thing to do is nothing," I declared, "because we are well on the way to destruction as a people." And then I asked a question: "But if we do want to survive as a people, what is it that was good about us?"

I let the comments sink in. There was a silence. I asked again: "What was it that was good about our people?"

I don't know whether that question had ever been asked. But its effect was immediate and extraordinary, provoking a palpable stirring of the Iñupiaq spirit as our people began to put into words the qualities that had been instilled in us over untold generations.

As our people spoke, I jotted down the qualities they described on a piece of paper mounted on an easel. The words and phrases were probably obvious to the elders among us in the room. But in that room, on that day, they were seriously contemplated for the first time by new generations. In many respects, that list represented the Iñupiaq version of the Ten Commandments.

I wrote until people stopped speaking:

- Knowledge of language
- Sharing
- Respect for others
- Cooperation
- Respect for elders
- Love for children
- Hard work
- Knowledge of family tree
- Avoidance of conflict
- Respect for nature
- Spirituality
- Humor
- Family roles
- Hunter success
- Domestic skills
- Humility
- Responsibility to tribe

During my retreat at Ivik, I had realized that one of the key problems was that we were no longer identifying ourselves as a people. As we had become increasingly individualized in our perceptions and actions, we had begun to identify ourselves with institutions from outside our culture. That was creating conflicts among us that had never before existed. For example, there were now Iñupiaq Republicans and Iñupiaq Democrats, Iñupiaq Catholics, Baptists, and Mormons. Our lives were affected and influenced to varying degrees by the tribe, the borough, the village corporation, the regional corporation, the school district, and the regional nonprofit. All of these institutions added to the complexity of life, and we had no overriding way to perceive and understand them in relation to who we were—the Iñupiaq people.

In the face of the great changes that were engulfing us, it was essential that we become unified again. We needed to recover our sense of commonality.

By the end of the meeting, the people in that room clearly saw that the values we had listed exemplified the best qualities of the Iñupiaq people. We had managed to capture the essence of our special way of life. All who attended now had a standard by which they could measure their lives and the institutions to which they were connected. Rather than lash out at institutions—the schools, for instance—we could now use the Iñupiaq values as a positive basis for changing the institutions so that they helped reinforce our children's identity.

We now could see more clearly the morass we had been in. But we could also see a ray of light—a way out of this mess. Indeed, for the first time, we began to recognize and celebrate how much of great value we had, despite the ravages of change and repression.

We had our land. We had managed to get our country to let us keep more than two million acres of territory rich in fish and game and Iñupiaq history.

We had our language. In spite of the school system that had tried to beat it out of us, and in spite of the fact that many of us spoke Iñupiaq in only a bumbling fashion, the richness of the language still lived, and it still could be passed along to our children and grandchildren.

We were interconnected in a way few modern people can claim to be. Our bloodlines were strong, if somewhat confused, and the ancient ties of iḷavut, family, were honored even among the modern generations.

Our art and music and dance survived, having somehow outlived the missionaries who had declared it sinful to dance for joy and to celebrate life with the drum.

Most important, the values that emerged from that meeting in Kotzebue were seen by all to be unimpeachable. We had managed to transcend the divisions that had been tearing us apart in the various institutions we represented. We had come to absolute agreement that these were our core values, our people's best qualities. They had enabled us to survive the great challenges of life in the Arctic and they were still critical today and for the future. They had allowed us to cross over from the ancient world to the modern, without obliterating our identity in the process. They had allowed us to keep the best of the old world as we sought to survive in the tumultuous new order.

To me, the beauty of what became known as Iñupiat Iḷitqusiat—Iñupiat Values—was the fact that they were not material. They were deeply entrenched in the mind and heart and spirit, and entirely transportable. You can be anywhere in the world and retain your Iñupiaq identity and values. You can pursue the highest academic credentials and become as wealthy as Bill Gates and still be the Iñupiaq of whom your forefathers would be proud.

The meeting in the Senior Center brought joy, relief, and a rejuvenation of the Iñupiaq spirit. We had agreed upon the ancient values that we must now infuse into the school curriculum, into the ways the tribe and the corporation do business, into the message of the churches and other institutions. We now had a means to reinforce who we are.

With little delay, we set about calling village meetings to share our experience in Kotzebue. Elders and local leaders in all eleven villages in the region participated. Iñupiaq Spirit Committees began to develop programs of cultural renewal that fit each locality.

In all the years I spent working in the Alaska Native community, this was the most rewarding effort—and the most difficult—I had ever undertaken. When it comes to the renewal of identity, spirit, language, and values, there are no panaceas. It takes concentration and work.

Just as the nuns and the monks and the priests have to focus on prayer and retreat, day after day and year after year, to stay on the straight and narrow—our own people have to similarly commit themselves to the task of preserving their continuity through a dedication to the language, the music, the arts, the knowledge of our land, and the values that make them unique.

In 1980, I spoke to the Alaska Federation of Natives convention on behalf of the NANA region and made a point of telling the two thousand delegates about my time in Nome, the initial despair, and the path we eventually found to reinforce ourselves and our people. Since then, many villages and regions have developed spirit camps and used the Iñupiat Values as a guide in their efforts to rejuvenate their own spirit. Some concentrate on the reintroduction of ancient dances and songs of joy, others focus on language or on the rich history and geography in their homelands. In the NANA region, we developed Camp Sivuuniiġvik ("a place to plan for the future") as a place for young Iñupiat to go to maintain their language and culture and to meet other youngsters from the Indiana-sized region of eleven villages. Here they interact with elders, they fish, butcher seals, learn legends. We have also worked with Rosetta Stone's Endangered Language Program to develop an introductory Iñupiaq language disc for use by anyone interested in learning our language. The Chugach Region in the Gulf of Alaska—a region that had been under the control of the Russians during the 1800s—has resurrected an abandoned village called Nuchek as a spirit camp that is used in the summer months for both children and adults. One of the great challenges before us is to instill the will in our people to require our schools to use the knowledge inherent in our elders to help our children reconnect with their homeland and their history.

The rage of my youth was rooted in ignorance of my history. I did not understand the colonial mentality. I knew nothing about the role of religion in controlling human beings in areas beyond the spiritual—in our case, the predation on family ties, the denigration of our language and cultural practices. I didn't know about economic oppression and advantage. I didn't know about class systems and snobbery. I didn't recognize the role of the classroom in obliterating cultural identity and traditional knowledge.

In the end, you have to understand the times you live in and the mentality of those whose decisions affect you. The missionaries had been motivated both by zealous self-righteousness and plain old dollar signs. To be fair, they worked hard to provide health care and sanitation and to set us on what they saw as the path to heaven. But they never really understood us, and abetted by the federal government, they made decisions that should have been made by our own people, using their power to repress our ability to govern ourselves. Our parents and grandparents acquiesced in all this, and "gave" us to the system in the belief that they were offering us a better life. What they didn't understand was that it was possible to retain our souls, our identity, our culture, and still pick up enough of the Western ways to flourish in the new order.

Iñupiat Iḷitqusiat opened my eyes. Now we had a new way of looking at our continuing struggle. It wasn't enough to claim our lands, we had to claim our ways of thinking, acting, and living—the ways my mother Naunġaġiaq and her elderly friends and relations instilled in me, and that taught me patience, the ability to withstand pain and deprivation without self-pity, and the camaraderie of common effort. This was the true spirit of our people, and this was what was being resurrected.

We are the descendants of people who learned to take what the conditions offered us and thrive. That was the spirit that guided our families, clans, tribes, and nations. It is a spiritual force, deeply embedded in our people, and it is just as important in the rapidly changing world we now inhabit as it was when all Alyeska belonged to Native peoples.

The stronger our identity and spirit, the stronger the likelihood that we will keep our land for future generations.

Iñupiat Iḷitqusiat must not be allowed to fade.

Our elders and our grandchildren are counting on us.

Epilogue

My birth mother, Makpiiq, once told a story about the first time an airplane came. On a clear, blue-sky winter afternoon, people were going about their normal work and play in the village when someone noticed, high in the sky, a silver object gleaming in the afternoon sun. As the villagers watched, the object grew brighter and brighter, closer and larger. Nothing like this had ever been seen before, and this blinding object reminded them of the story they had been told of the Lord who was to return to earth and cause the good to rise to heaven and the bad to fall into a fiery hell. People became frantic and ran in all directions, wailing, *"Aachikkaŋ! Tuquni-aqtugut!"* (I'm scared! We're going to die!). All thought that this was the end of the world as this object—a hundred times larger than the swans—swooped down and alit on the river ice below the village with the loudest, most piercing sound they had ever heard. All of a sudden it was deathly quiet, with just the hint of a breeze rustling the willows and trees.

A lone human being dressed in heavy clothes and a tight-fitting hat with huge goggle-eyes stepped out of the object and looked around. The only brave ones were the children, who warily shuffled up to the object and peered inside to see what made it fly. After a few minutes of staring at the dials in front, one of the children bravely announced her conclusion: *"Tuqtuqtuurat! Tuqtuqtuurat!"* (The clocks make it fly!)

The Iñupiat took quickly to the notion of flying to cover the vast distances of our homeland, and I am no exception. Ever since my first memorable flight from Nome to Kotzebue, I have done the same thing: when nearing Kotzebue, I begin craning my neck to view the homeland of the Qikiqtaġrugmiut, punctuated by the forty-mile-long peninsula bounded by Kotzebue Sound and Hotham Inlet. Ignoring the stomach-churning bounce over the Arctic Circle (a stunt the pilots pull off for the benefit of tourists), I try to spy the villages of Selawik, Noorvik, and Kiana and to pick out other landmarks—the Kobuk, Noatak, and Selawik Rivers, Ivik, Pipe Spit, the ancient trading place of Sisaulik and especially Ikkattuq, where I spent my early life. This is the homeland that is etched in my memory.

Almost always, there is someone on the plane heading home to attend the funeral of a loved one. I have been one of those and now find myself, oddly enough, almost an elder. In my lifetime, Aqpayuk and Nauŋġaġiaq, Unaliiqutaq, Tiliiktaq, Iġvaluk, Umiivik, Saqik, Auleniq, Niŋaugagraq, Aġnaġaq, Saigulik, Makpiiq, and many others have passed into eternity. The people of our villages are almost all related in one way or another. Despite absences that sometimes last for decades, the deceased often are brought home for their final farewell, and elders, relatives, and even strangers come by to pay their respects, to help dig the graves in the rock-hard permafrost, to sing and make a comment or to deliver pots of caribou stew for the potluck. That is one of the beauties of our world that brings me to tears.

Cemeteries, in our part of the world, are difficult to maintain. The graves are usually in ground that is permanently frozen but near the surface, the ground thaws and re-refreezes, and the little fences and crosses that mark graves eventually lean and rot and fall apart. In the old days, the practice was to place the body of the deceased on a wooden platform, surrounded by his tools and hunting implements, and eventually the remains became a part of the natural universe and the memory of a loved one was carried in the hearts of the living. For us, the idea of burial and of permanent markers is relatively recent—as is so much else in our world.

Having lived amid such constant and unpredictable change, the one rock for me has been the love and compassion of Naungaġiaq and the family in which I was reared and the natural environment of the little universe imprinted in me as a youngster.

I was raised among people who today would be considered poverty-stricken. In the 1940 United States Census, they noted that our household's valuables consisted of a sixteen-by-eighteen-foot log home worth $250, three nets ($15), ten traps ($7), ten dogs ($200). The annual income of the whole combined family was $500, and the seals, berries, ducks, salmon, and other fish we had stored for food were valued at $375. Our net worth came to a grand total of $1,347.

Even so, in spite of the paucity of material goods, we lived a life of excitement. No one day was the same as the previous one. We were always on the move, interacting with one another and with other families. We were an integral part of the land, traveling in harmony with the seasons and the migration of nature's gifts. We placed ourselves in the vicinity of the creatures that allowed us to thrive. We had to work for it, and that was the challenge. Quite often nature turned against us and the struggle then began in earnest until the season changed or the caribou, fish, or seals returned.

The land and the family, the thousands of years of continuity, still pull us homeward just as if there were an invisible rubber band snapping us back to the land our forefathers roamed. Despite painful memories, despite the fact that hunger, cold, and outright drudgery drove many of us out to an easier living, the innocence of the old way of life is permanently etched in our sensibilities. The big one you missed, the lucky shot, the worst blizzard you endured, the albino caribou, the year of plentiful berries, your first baby, and the fine muskrat parka your mother made, the time so-and-so missed the blanket during *nalukataq* (blanket toss).

Now you taste the sweetness of salmonberries, the richness of *akutuq* (Eskimo ice cream), the delicate fresh seal oil with *mipkuq* (dried seal meat), *iŋaluat* (dried intestines), fresh duck soup, and *màktak* (whale skin with blubber). It's almost enough to make you cry just thinking of it all and the family and friends with whom you will share the occasion—the wordplay and put-downs and recollections of funny occasions.

In this world, no matter what you may have done Outside, you are still the same person you always were to everyone. You might have discovered how to create gold or you might have become the most powerful man in Schenectady over the years you were away, but here, you are who you were. Your accomplishments are measured by your character and the qualities long and deeply prized in the region. Up here, humility and cooperation, generosity and goodwill still trump wealth and academic and political prowess.

The bonds of language, shared cultural ties, and common

understanding of geography and flora and fauna are still defining qualities of our people. When these qualities disappear, we as a people begin to disappear. We become strangers in our own land.

Ever since we first got tobacco from the Russians, along with coffee and tea, pots and pans, and matches, knives, and telescopes, we have been changing. We changed when the whalers brought alcohol and guns. We changed when the epidemics of flu and diphtheria and tuberculosis swept our villages. We changed with the Gold Rush. We changed when the missionaries and government combined to control our families, our culture, our very spirit. We changed with the arrival of airplanes, motors, telephones, and television. We changed with the arrival of statehood. We've changed with the divvying up of our natural world between federal, state, and Native landholdings and the arrival of corporations.

In my earlier life, I privately thought that I was the only one suffering all this confusion of identity and place. I had been set adrift from the old life and had to swim upstream in strange waters. Over many years, I began to understand that I was not at all alone. I saw how as members of minorities in Alaska and in America we didn't make the rules but we were expected to live by the rules. Our situation was universal. Conquering forces arrived on foreign shores and took it for granted that they had the right to control the spaces once occupied by a multitude of indigenous peoples. It's not unlike invasive species of all kinds. And like all living things, once invaded, the cultures being displaced have to modify their own lives and ways in order to survive. In America's early days, for example, the Indians were eventually forced to live by the law of those who had the guns. They became a captive and dependent people.

I saw how the knowledge Native people derived through trial and error over untold millennia was crowded out by new knowledge, new ways of thinking. When that old knowledge disappears, along with the sense of community and the dedication to the common welfare, confusion begins to reign. People grow disconnected from their language and culture, family relationships grow weaker, and eventually individuals live in relative isolation. Some people call that freedom. But when I was growing up, there was a conspicuous effort in our communities to keep people from becoming isolated and self-absorbed. I think our culture recognized the dangers of losing human contact and warmth, crucial qualities for sanity and emotional strength in a place like the Arctic.

I thought of the millions of immigrants who came to this great land to build a new life and escape the strictures, poverty, controls, and terrorism they might have faced in their own homelands. In this case, they had made a conscious decision to change—in many cases, gratefully. Others intended to hang on as hard as they could to those qualities that made them unique. Right off the bat, they were treated as the Indians had been. Someone gave them new, more pronounceable names. They were encouraged to give up their traditions and fashions and were told to learn English. They were given shovels or mops and paid little for backbreaking work. In the meantime, they were discriminated against and told how to vote and called all manner of nasty names.

As I grew to understand all this, things began to fall into place. I didn't approve of what had happened to us, but there was some comfort in knowing that we weren't the only ones who had suffered such calamities. All of a sudden, rather than seeing us living in hell, I began to see that despite the ravages of time and custom on our people and our traditions, we still lived in a heaven on earth.

It became clear to me that our old world was harsh but wonderful, and that today, that awesome, pristine world still exists, as do the excellent qualities of our people. Few places in America are like Alaska, where sparkling rivers and streams will never be dammed and sprawling valleys will never see a superhighway or a McDonald's sign. It is a place where countless natural geographical points maintain names that go far into the mists of time, full of meaning and still connected to the people who reside there today. By contrast, in my occasional visits to places like Nantucket and Martha's Vineyard, I see wonderful, ancient Indian place names that carry no message at all to those who live there today; the fact that there was a world of human activity and drama— lovers' quarrels, tribal warfare, trade ceremonies, games, and religious rituals—goes unnoticed because the people who named the places are long gone.

I often wonder what might have happened in our world had we been more aware of the catastrophes faced by our fellow indigenous peoples, beginning in Jamestown four hundred years ago. Would our great-grandfathers have tried to control our space and the rules within that space? Would life have been better for us? Could we have forestalled the negative effects of disease, alcohol, starvation, and people with superiority complexes? Would we now have rules that would blend with our traditional ways in the dispensation of welfare, rules of inheritance, violations of norms, and the rules of hunting and fishing? Could we have provided an education built on the knowledge imprinted in the minds of our people from generations past rather than summarily rejecting our traditions as useless for the future of our children? What would have happened if we had been able to benefit from the vast resources now being harvested by multinational corporations from the lands we no longer control?

We now hold only 16 percent of Alaska's vast territory. But that 16 percent is precious. It is reassuring to know that for our future generations, we have held on to the space that nurtured our existence and we have the opportunity to hold it for all time to come.

The key is to maintain our identity, our values, and our spirit. And the key to accomplishing that is in the hands of individuals, families, clans, and the elders for whom we fought so hard. Every one of us has a Naunġaġiaq in our lives, someone who gave us all he or she had. Our challenge is to preserve the memory of those who sustained us and to conserve and protect the land that fostered their time on Earth.

In the frozen dark of a winter morning, back in the *ivrulik*, my mother Naunġaġiaq would wake early and quickly pull on a parka to protect her from the chill. She then sat silently on her caribou *qaatchiaq*, staring off into the distance, lost in thoughts she never put into words.

Similarly, on a summer evening near the beach, after a day crammed full of the constant work it took to keep us all alive, Naunġaġiaq would grow quiet and gaze out at the crimson sun setting across the bay. Once again, she seemed to detach herself spiritually from the everyday world.

I presume that she was praying at moments like these. She was among the first generation of Christians in Kotzebue, converted by the Quakers, and perhaps she was praying to the Christian God. But she also used to speak of *siḷa*, our traditional word for the forces of nature that create weather. Maybe, during these contemplative moments, my mother also spoke to her own great spirits, those of the Iñupiaq universe.

How I wish that I could speak to Nauṅaġiaq and Aqpayuk today. I would like to hear from them how they felt about the transformations they experienced in their lifetime. I would like to know how they felt as they moved from the old world of many spirits to the new world of Christian belief. I would like to understand what they really thought about the missionaries and the schools, the traders and the government bureaucrats, the future of their children and our people.

Their generation was the first to try to make sense of the new world that was enveloping our people. There is so much I could learn from them, if only I could ask.

But this I know without any question: the spirit of Nauṅaġiaq and Aqpayuk and others of the old world envelop and sustain me as they always have, even when I am far from home. It has been that way ever since I left Kotzebue at the age of fifteen. Truly, the elders of our old world provided a kind of unconditional love that helped us to maintain our humanity, and it was that love that provided ballast for me and my generation as we began to feel the full force of the change that overtook us.

It was the time they took to teach us through their everyday activity. It was the stories they told, the encouragement they gave so generously. It was the patience and endurance they always showed, no matter what effort was required—physical or spiritual—whether it was trudging long distances across the ice or tundra or taking care of any family member who needed their help and sustenance.

I can still see Naung̣ag̣iaq as she paused, sitting on her *qaatchiaq* or contemplating the sunset, to check in to the world of the spirits. No matter how much our circumstances change, I hope our people will always stop from time to time to do the same, to renew the bonds that connect us across five hundred generations.

Iñupiaq: The Language and the People

Many indigenous people call themselves "the People" in their own language. In the case of the Iñuit in Alaska, we refer to ourselves as "Iñupiat," the Real People. Iñuit is our term for "humans." "Iñupiaq" is our term for our language as well as our identity. There are variations in the language among villages just dozens of miles apart. On the other hand, many root words are common all the way from the Bering Strait to Greenland and in between—the Northwest Territories in Canada as well as in Nunavut, in Quebec as well as in Labrador.

Our language is related to the Yupik language in southwestern Alaska, or as we call it, "the Delta"—meaning the delta of the Yukon and Kuskokwim rivers. It's odd that we are more conversant with the Iñuit in eastern Canada and Greenland than we are with our Yupik neighbors just a few hundred miles to the south of us in Alaska.

According to Wikipedia, "The traditional language of the Iñuit is a system of closely interrelated dialects that are not readily comprehensible from one end of the Iñuit world to the other, and some people do not think of it as a single language but rather as a group of languages." The reality is that in my visits to Greenland during the early years of the Iñuit Circumpolar Conference, I was overjoyed to be able to communicate with the Iñuit living there despite my Iñupiaq-speaking limitations. They had the good fortune of being able to write their language and didn't have the fierce cultural repression we experienced in our schools in Alaska.

Oddly enough, in the Iñupiaq language where I come from in northwest Alaska, we say *iñuit* for "human beings." In the Yupik language, it is pronounced "yu-it." Our word for "person" is *Iñuk* and their word is *yuk*. My humorous response to my Yupik friends is that they just aren't *in* like we are. The good news for the Yupik is that they have hung on to their language more successfully than we have in our part of Alaska. According to Dr. Michael Krauss, the former head of the Alaska Native Language Center at the University of Alaska, "Yupik is in the best shape of all Alaskan languages," and the Iñupiaq language "will be practically extinct in Alaska by the end of this century . . . *unless* Iñupiaq as a Second Language programs flourish." He blames No Child Left Behind laws that leave no room for indigenous languages, as well as the influence of TV, English-only pressures, and other media for the decline of these beautiful languages.

In our language we have several words for "snow" that denote a variety of meanings: *apun* is the generic word for snow, but we also have the word *aniu*. Snow that is crystallized and laden with fresh water is called *arriq*. When the wind is blowing close to the ground, the snow blowing with it is called *natiġvik*, from the word *natiq*, our word for "floor." If it is snowing in a gentle way, we call it *qannik*.

Our generic word for ice is *siku*. If it is ice that was formed overnight, it is called *siklak*. The multiple-year ice is called *tiqaluyaq*, and *ivu* is ice that has been rolled or pushed up by pressures in the ocean. These pressure ridges can go on for miles and miles and on occasion can threaten communities along the shore.

Many words we use come from trading with the Natives from across the Bering Strait who brought us the goods we began to crave because they made life easier and more exciting. The Yupik people use the word *kuufiaq* for "coffee," from the Russian *koffye*. By the time it reached Kotzebue, it morphed into *kuupiaq*. We use the word *mukaaq*, from the Russian *muka*, for "flour." From the Russian word for "tea," *chai*, we use the word *saigu*, and farther south they use the word *chaiu*.

The use of many of these words goes so far back in time we had begun to think they were Iñupiaq in origin.

Sometimes a matter of emphasis creates totally different meanings in a word. We have a word for "rear end" which completely changes the meaning if you don't say it right. *Iqquq* means "butt" or "rear end," with the emphasis strongly on the *Iq*. If it is pronounced with both syllables evenly stressed, it means "to wipe" the rear end. Likewise, our word for a "stopping place" or hotel is *nullaġvik*, and the word for "a place to lie down" is *nallaġvik*.

There are just a few sounds in Iñupiaq that are not used in English. One is the guttural *g* sound, as in my name, Iġġiaġruk. In the Iñupiaq font, it is a dotted *ġ*.

Another unusual sound is a rolling *l* (*lia*), as in the word *iḷiak*, meaning "tangled," as in a tangled hair mass. That *ḷ* has a dot under it. Another unusual feature of our language is that our word for "fire" is *ikniq*, similar to the word "ignite," and the word for "stove" is *iknigvik*—"a place where ignition is occurring."

Meanings are changed by the addition of sounds to the basic word. Once we were traveling in the NANA region villages encouraging each to come up with its own program of cultural rejuvenation. In Kobuk (a corruption of *kuuqpak*, meaning "big river"), the smallest village in our region, the people considered using one suggestion by an elderly resident as a name for their program: the recommendation was *alġaqruu ŋuralaḷiqraŋatigun*. Roughly, the translation was "the methodology and means of encouraging proper behavior, occasionally," the root word being *alġaqsruq*, meaning "prompting proper behavior."

Iñupiaq Glossary

A

aachikkaŋ!   what a narrow escape! look out! I'm scared!

aana   grandmother; great-aunt

aapaiḷaurat   children without a father; singular: *aapaiḷauraq*

aglagiagiñ!   go to school!

aglagiaqtugut   we go to school

aglak   a letter character; to write

aġviq   bowhead whale

aksrak   to haul

aksraktautit   car or truck

akutuq   Eskimo ice cream (a mixture of whipped caribou fat and berries, meat, or fish)

anaġvik   toilet, outhouse

anaktaq   to participate in competitive games; to compete in sports

anaq   excrement, feces

anigniq   the breath of life

aŋalatchi   to manage, be in charge of

aŋalatchirugut   we are managing

aŋatkuq   shaman

aŋuyak   to wage war; battle

aŋuyaktugut   we are at war

aqargit   ptarmigan

arguaŋa   to be audacious, bold, aggressive

arguaŋaruaq   the bold, aggressive one

ataata   grandfather

atautchikuaq   to go together, united as one

atikluk   a colorful, hooded fabric parka, usually for inside use or for warm summer days

ausaq   to go over there, cross, e.g., a river, a street, or a body of water; to go to the Lower Forty-eight or to Europe

ausaaqtuŋa   I go outside to the Lower Forty-eight

aviŋaq or *aviŋauraq*   mouse

I

Iġġich Isuat   the end of the mountains

iġitchaq   to pluck feathers

ikaiyqti   helper

ikkat   to be shallow, e.g., a body of water

ikkattuq   it is shallow

ikuun   scraper for animal skin; wood plane

iḷa   relative by blood, marriage, or name; part of a whole; companion, friend, partner

iḷatka   my relatives; family

iḷavut   our families, our relatives

iliktaq   roasted flour

iḷitqusiat   their spirit

iḷitqusiq   spirit

inisaq   meat rack

iŋaluat   small intestines of human and land animals

Iñuit   people

Iñuk   person

Iñupiat   north Alaskan Eskimos

Iñupiat Iḷitqusiat   The Spirit of the Iñupiat

iñuuniaq   to be life-giving; to live off the land

itchuq   to await prey behind a blind

Itqiḷiq   Indian

itraliq   to be extremely cold (of weather)
ivik   grass
ivrulik   sod house

K

kakkaaq   to starve to death
kakkaaqtut   they starve to death
kamiks   boots made of whale skin
katima   to have, hold a meeting
katimarut   they are holding a meeting
kigun   tooth
kigutinŋu   to have a toothache
kiiġvik   cutting board
kiikka!   go ahead! let's go!
kiiki!   keep it up, you asked for it, you do not deserve any pity or sympathy!
kiita!   let's go!
kikmiññaq   lowbush cranberry

M

maktak   whale skin with blubber
manik   money
mauliġauraq   to play jumping from one piece of ice to another
mauliq   to miss the piece of ice and sink suddenly
miġiaq   vomit
mipkuq   dried bearded-seal meat

N

natchiq   hair seal
nakmaġvik   hunting bag
nakmauti   a specially made pack of sealskin or canvas with pouches on the sides that fits over a dog's back
nakuu   be good, nice
nakuuruq   it is good

naluaġmiut   white persons

naluaġmiutaq   item of the white person, white person's food

naluaq   sun-bleached seal or bearded-seal skin

nalukataq   whaling festival held (usually in June) after spring whaling season ends; also, a blanket toss

naniq   light, lamp

naniqaqtugut!   we have light!

natmaun or *natmauti*   dog pack; backpack

navraaq   artifact, something discovered while digging

navraaqtuq!   he found an artifact!

niqipiaq or *niqi*   meat (literally "real food")

nuiaqpalik   a mermaidlike creature

nuna   land, earth

nunamun   to the land

nunavut   our lands

P

patiq   marrow

pigaaq   to stay up late

piyaquq   to have an accident, be injured in an accident

piyaquġuktuq   he is accident-prone

puttuqsri   to understand, comprehend, realize

puttuqsriruŋa   I come to a realization

puya   grime, dirt, sticky oil, seal-oil residue

Q

qaatchiaq   skin mattress

qanitchaq   entryway, storm shed, cold porch (to the house)

qaqisaq   brain

qaqqulaaq   pilot bread, cracker

qauġri   to gain consciousness; become aware of one's surroundings

qayusaaq   cooked cranberries

qia   to cry, shed tears

qianak!   don't cry!

qikiqtaġruk   peninsula

Qikiqtaġruk   Kotzebue, Alaska

qiŋak   nose, referring to a hole in the sod roof of an *ivrulik*, which is fitted with a short hollow log and allows the structure to breathe

qitiktuaq   to play games, be involved in recreation

qitiktuaqtugut   we play games

qiuġvik   wooden board for scraping hair from animal skin, for cutting leather

qivit   to go off in a huff, leave indignantly, give up

quaġaq   sour dock, sour grass, sorrel

quaq   raw frozen meat or fish

quiagipsi apai   I thank you very much

S

sakuuk   to work very hard, overwork

sakuuktuŋa   I am working hard

sanik   dust, lint; caribou hair on clothing or floor

sanŋit   (plural form of *sanik*) leaves mixed in with wild berries

siġluaq   underground ice or food cellar

sila   weather; atmosphere; air

sivutmun or *sivunmun*   forward, to the future

sukat   to be fast, speedy

sukattuq   it is fast

suli   and furthermore; also; still in progress

T

tigu   to take hold and hang on

tigulugu!   claim it!

tigummiuŋ!   hold on to it!

tumi isua   the end of the trail

tuqtuqtuuraq   clock

tuqtuqtuurat   clocks

tuqu   to die

tuquniaqtugut   we will die

tuvaaqqan   companion, mate, partner; spouse

tuaaqatiga   my companion, my spouse

tupsi   a strap that ties around a mother's waist and holds a baby upright

tuuq   ice chisel, ice pick

U

ugruk   bearded seal

ukpik   snowy owl

ulit   the earth had turned inside out

ulu   Iñupiaq woman's crescent-shaped knife

umialik   whaling captain; rich person (literally "the one with a boat")

umiaqpak   ship

umiat   skin boats

uqsruq   seal oil, fuel

utiq   to return, go back

utiqtuŋa   I return

utiqtuŋa nunamun   I return to the land

utniq   hairless skin, sometimes used to describe fermented flippers, a
   delicacy

utraq or *urraq*   fermented meat (usually walrus flipper; walrus skin
   with blubber; bearded-seal flipper; or whale flippers), eaten as a
   delicacy

Acknowledgments

For millennia, people who live in the Arctic have acknowledged that life is not possible without cooperative effort and generosity of spirit. It is true in my own life, and this book would have not been possible without the help and support of many people.

My immediate family—Abbe and our children, Priscilla, Mollie, James, and Elizabeth—who provided love and encouragement and who were awakened at all hours of the night to hear me read a piece I had just written. Jim Aqpayuk Labelle, my brother, who provided a willing ear at odd hours. Dick and Opal Miller, who cared for me in those early days. Marge and Bob Baker, who gave me a roof when there was none. Edith Bullock, who provided a job and encouragement when I decided to attend George Washington University. Justice Jay Rabinowitz, who taught me constitutional law and provided the opportunity to study Native land claims in Alaska. Reva Wulf Shircel and Ruby Tansy John, who listened to me at the University of Alaska and believed in the land rights of Alaska Natives. Emil Notti, who shared with me the pressures of the early efforts to organize the Alaska Federation of Natives and to protect Native lands. Stewart Udall, who as Secretary of the Interior had the backbone to freeze land transactions in Alaska until Congress could pass the land claims settlement bill. Alice Rogoff Rubenstein, who strongly encouraged me to tell my story. Susan Mercandetti, who critiqued my early efforts to write and gave me encouragement. Merrill McLoughlin, who, in her quiet way, provided structure for my stories and recollections. Kris Dahl, my agent, who believed there was a place for my story in the world of books. Edna Ahgeak MacLean, who checked my Iñupiaq language. Oliver Aviugana Leavitt, my Barrow buddy who provided insight. My nephew Pete Tarruq Schaeffer and his wife, Polly Aġniq Schaeffer, who fed me *niqipiaq* (real food) and gave me a bed at Ivik, away from the maddening crowd. Sarah Crichton, my editor, who astounded me by taking a risk on an unknown quantity and who believed that the public should hear the story of a little-known part of America.

Index